ETHEL ENNIS

ETHEL ENNIS

The Reluctant Jazz Star

An Illustrated Biography
by Sallie Kravetz

 GATEWAY PRESS INC./Baltimore
HUGHES ENTERPRISES   1984

Manufactured in the United States of America

FIRST EDITION

Hughes Enterprises/A Division of Gateway Press, Inc.
1001 N. Calvert Street
Baltimore, MD 21202

Library of Congress Cataloging in Publication Data

Kravetz, Sallie, 1939-
   Ethel Ennis, the reluctant jazz star.

   Bibliography: p.
   Discography: p.
   1. Ennis, Ethel, 1932-   .   2 Singers—United
States—Biography.
   ML420.E65K7 1984   784.5 [B]   84-80200

International Standard Book Number 0-9614053-0-9

Calligraphy by Nadia Hlibka

Typesetting by Superior Composition Co.

Front cover photo by Sallie Kravetz

We gratefully acknowledge:
Alfred A. Knopf, Inc. for the use of the quote from *Tao Te Ching* by Lao Tsu. Translated by Gia-Fu Feng and Jane English. © 1972.

In loving memory of

my dad, Mack Kravetz,

one of the best

sax players around

Contents

Preface

This book is the story of the life and times of a jazz singer (though she doesn't like to classify herself as such) named Ethel Ennis. It is also the story of a woman who was headed for stardom and who, in the fifty-ninth minute of the hour of her breakthrough, decided to return home to examine her life. This self-examination would eventually come to occupy the next two decades of her life. The writing of this book would become the opportunity for Ethel to reveal what she had discovered during those last two decades.

For me, the author and a close confidant of Ethel, the realization of this project represents nothing short of a miracle. Shortly after I left my career as a media educator in the Anne Arundel County School System, I was faced with the pressing question, "What do I want to do with my life?" Although I had some ambitious schemes, the fact was that I was afraid to state the truth, because at the time, what I really wanted seemed impossible. Finally one day in a conversation with a friend I blurted it out, "What I really want is to use my photographic skills and my ability to communicate in order to make a difference in people's lives. I mean what I really want is to have my work in a book." After I said it, I thought, "How absurd of me. Countless people have that dream. My chances are probably one in a million." And I promptly tried to forget that I had said it.

In the meantime I had worked closely with Ethel for nearly ten years on various projects: photographs, a video documentary, a concert production, as a member of her production company ENE, and just prior to this book, on a scholarly research project when I studied Ethnomusicology at the University of Maryland, Baltimore County. I thought I really knew Ethel—but I didn't. While engaging in all of the projects, I was inexplicably haunted by a nagging question: "What really is the truth about Ethel Ennis' career?" In my most secret thoughts I felt that Ethel had been given more opportunities than most of us and that somehow she had failed. Something about Ethel's story seemed murky to me. The facts as I knew them just didn't seem to jibe.

At the same time, during the past five years, along with hundreds of thousands of others, I had been doing a little self-examination of my own and was involved in programs that addressed a much broader question, namely, "What would my life be like if I brought myself, who I am, fully into the world—if I evolved myself to the highest level of my being?" Some of the discoveries that I was making caused me to become even more suspicious as I replayed things Ethel had told me.

A lot of what she had said to me began to sound like some kind of trumped up excuse. I began to learn that in living life we either have the results that we say we want or all of the excuses and reasons why we don't. And I for one wanted to have the results and not the excuses.

All of these thoughts were mulling around in my mind when divine inspiration came along and said, "Hey, wake up. There's an opportunity staring you in the face. What about your photographs of Ethel? What about the opening of Ethel's Place? Go for it." I thought about this and I knew that Ethel's new cabaret theater, Ethel's Place, was moving toward construction and that there would be a renewed interest in Ethel Ennis. I considered that perhaps my photographic documentation of various moments in Ethel's life would be publishable. So I picked up the Baltimore *Yellow Pages* and opened to "P" for publishers. I went through the list and made three phone calls and got nowhere—but at number four, something clicked.

I spoke with an engaging woman named Ann Hughes at Gateway Press, a division of Genealogical Publishing Company. During the course of the conversation we discovered that we had shared a common experience. Both of us had taken the est training, the program alluded to earlier. While that news was exciting, it didn't immediately result in my having found a publisher, since Gateway ordinarily works with authors of family history books who pay the production costs and market their own books. So that seemed to be the end of that—until the next day. As I prepared to walk out the door, Ann called back and said, "I went home last night and thought about what you said. I have some money to invest and I think this could be a fun project so I may be willing to take myself on as Gateway's client. Let's meet and talk about it." I was stunned. Not only that—Ann had never heard of Ethel Ennis, so I knew it was strictly on my own merits that she would be talking to me and not because a friend of mine had a "name" in Baltimore—though that would prove to be valuable later on.

And that was the beginning of the miracle: the realization that when one declares what one truly wants in life, and goes for the possibility, that somehow it can happen. The other part of the miracle was learning to trust the process of creative unfoldment. The fact that the book evolved as it did is a demonstration of that. At first it was to be a coffee-table type photography book with lots of gorgeously reproduced photographs—but that was a short-lived ego trip. I saw that what really might make a difference in people's lives would be to use the Ethel Ennis story as a vehicle to explore some fundamental questions about life. And Ethel's life provided a rich storehouse for just such an exploration—issues about success and failure, show business, artistic integrity, racial prejudice, discrimination against women, interracial marriage, popular music, jazz, and spirituality could be examined within the context of Ethel's life.

Not only was Ethel herself the embodiment of these issues, she had saved the artifacts of having lived them. Stored away in boxes, bags, and envelopes was a gold mine of memories that she hadn't looked at for years, if ever. During the course of writing the book, we spent hundreds of hours digging around in Ethel's past like soul-searching archeologists. We brought old memories out of the darkness of the past and re-examined them in the new light of the present. Some nights we stayed up until nearly dawn sprawled on our hands and knees, hunched over pictures, newspaper clippings, old ads, magazine articles, and family albums which were strewn from one end of Ethel's living room to the other. We spent countless hours talking and sorting out these pieces of Ethel's life until they began to make some sense.

As we gathered together the reviews from the sixties, Ethel sometimes would stop and read what the critics had said about her performances back then. Usually it was something wonderful. Suddenly it dawned on me that this was the first time that Ethel had ever read these words of praise. I could see that she had no idea of how favorably her talent had been regarded in the past. Every once in a while I would notice a small glimmer of self-acknowledgement spread across her face—but she kept it low key as if she didn't want to appear to be too impressed with herself. It was similar to another occasion when I had recorded some leading jazz divas on a cassette and interspersed each one with an Ennis rendition. When I played it for Ethel and she heard first Sarah Vaughan immediately followed by Ethel Ennis, she said, "Oh, now I see why they were sayin' all that stuff about me soundin' like Sarah. I guess I really do in a way." That was in 1982, years after she had recorded those songs. She had never bothered to study herself during those earlier times. As for the memorabilia we rummaged through during those sleepless winter nights, the best of these precious, historic moments are now preserved for all time on the pages of this book.

Going through the process of creating this book and seeing it come to fruition has been a major breakthrough in my life—a true demonstration of what being committed can produce. But I clearly did not do it alone—and now that it's finished the best part for me is to publicly acknowledge all of those people in my life who have supported this project and my well-being in a multitude of ways during the past year. They are as follows: Ann Hughes, for trusting me; Ethel and Earl, for their love—no matter what; my "Course in Miracles" group for suffering through the process with me; the hundreds of people in my "Education for Living" seminars and Werner Erhard for creating the est training; my brother-in-law Marvin Sober for his *mitzvohs,* and of course, Marsha my sister, Blanche my mom and Rags my dog just for being there; and Phyllis Steinberg, Ed Rosen,

David Lehman, Patti Perskie, Hazel Chung, and Baron for believing in me even when I forgot to; and Charles Alpert for providing me with a way to make a living so that I could write the book.

Thanks also to Catherine Gilchrist at Blakeslee Lane for printing my photos; Nadia Hlibka for her beautiful, poetic calligraphy; Starr Belsky for polishing the manuscript; Joyce Graff, Bonnie Kunzel and David Lehman for reading the book, and Charlie Logan for learning to put up with my design ideas. And a special thanks to the Universal Power within us all.

Enjoy,

SALLIE KRAVETZ
Baltimore
1984

Fame or Self
which matters more

Self or Wealth
which is more precious

Gain or Loss
*which is more
painful*

—Lao Tsu

I God $Bless$ the $Child$

*E*THEL LLEWELLYN ENNIS, the future jazz singer, made her first appearance on this planet on November 28, 1932. However, there was no great spirit of joy or celebration to accompany her arrival. Arrabell and Andrew Ennis had recently buried one child, an infant named Arlene, and they hadn't yet paid for her funeral. During this current pregnancy, Bell, as she was called, thought about giving this baby up for adoption. She was looking at the cost of birth and the cost of death and times were hard.

No sooner had Ethel arrived than her life hung in the critical balance between cradle and coffin. She had a malady referred to by the family as "lazy liver." The symptoms were yellowing of the eyes and difficulty in breathing. Several days after her birth, a public health nurse appeared at the Ennis household. In those days, the Baltimore City Health Department routinely sent nurses to check on the health of newborns who had been birthed at home. Little did the nurse know that she was actually an angel of mercy in disguise. Ethel remembers hearing her maternal grandmother Honey telling the details years later.

"Honey told me that the nurse was a big German woman. She came to our third floor apartment at 525 North Calhoun Street where I was

1

layin' in my cradle—a dresser drawer lined with bedding. I was havin' trouble breathing so the nurse picked me up by the heels and started shakin' me and poundin' me on the back. She kept on shakin' and poundin' and shakin' and poundin' . . . ."

As the story goes, the nurse kept at this procedure for several time-arresting minutes, and finally there was an outburst of sound from the baby's lungs—the raw cry of life. It wasn't as melodic as the tones that Ethel would sing later on, but probably no sound would ever be more powerful. The nurse, the first white presence to enter Ethel's life, had done her job well. By the time she left, Bell and Andrew Ennis had let go of any thoughts of giving their baby up for adoption. Somehow they would make ends meet.

At the time, Ethel's father was a barber and was rarely at home. Despite having an artificial leg, he worked long hours at the shop on Harlem Avenue and was content to leave the child-rearing to Bell and her mother, the God-fearing, iron-willed Honey. Honey came from gutsy stock. Her own mother, Ethel's maternal great-grandmother, had lived in South Carolina as a slave. In due course she took the name of Eliza Garrison (the master's family name) and adopted Christianity. Once the slaves were freed, Eliza returned briefly to her homeland in Africa looking for the rest of her family. After an unsuccessful search, she returned as a free person to South Carolina and finished raising her family there.

Honey grew up, married, and with her husband moved to Baltimore where she gave birth to three daughters. Bell was the oldest and had the mildest manner of the three. The middle daughter Elizabeth, nicknamed "Sister," was a bit rebellious. Later in life she did a complete turnaround and became very devoted to the church. Sister moved away to New York early in Ethel's life, so Ethel barely grew to know her. Charlotte was the youngest, only two years older than Ethel and was the most rebellious of the three sisters. As Ethel and Charlotte grew up together, Charlotte acted out all of the things that Ethel herself would not dare to do. Ethel had a touch of rebelliousness, too, but she came across, on the surface at least, like the ideal "good little girl." And Mama and Honey made sure of that right from the start; little Ethel was raised with the *ultimate* in propriety. As Ethel remembers those days, she says, "I got a lot of care and a lot of attention. I was always properly dressed and groomed, properly cultivated. Once I was dressed, I couldn't go off the steps. It was, *You stay on those steps.* I couldn't visit my friends; I could only play with them in front of the house. I always obeyed."

Everything about Ethel's upbringing was determined by the church through Bell and Honey. They both sang in the church choir at Ames United Methodist Church. Bell was also the church organist and pianist.

In later years she went "on the road," traveling around playing piano and organ in Pentecostal, store front churches. At home Honey was the mouthpiece for the church. She served as the family matriarch and spiritual leader. If anyone was Ethel's guiding light, it was Honey. She instilled her strong religious values in Ethel's mind from the beginning. As Ethel says, "She talked about *The Bible* like those people were her neighbors. And it was always church, church, church . . . good, good, good. Churchlike meant ladylike to Honey. It was very important to her to make sure that I would grow up to be *a lady*. She would always say, 'Ladies don't do that,' whenever she caught me singin' at the table, whistlin', or snappin' my fingers while I was listenin' to music."

Honey's words falling on young Ethel's ears represented God Himself and even the devil. The church, on the other hand, was just a big brother. "I didn't understand why I had to go to church and I told myself that when I grew up, I wasn't gonna go!" As Ethel sees it today, Honey's imposing influence caused a basic dilemma. "In some ways her teachings kept me from being rowdy and gave me an air of sophistication. In other ways, they kept me from expressing myself from within."

Ethel's earliest memories go back to the little apartment on North Calhoun Street, especially to the front room. "It was a warm room. That's where all the heat, all the light, and all the action was. That was the room where I was taken care of." The Ennises rented their apartment from the Wise family. Their daughter Ethel Wise was Bell's contemporary and agreed to have the baby named after her. Big Ethel, as she was called after little Ethel came along, taught English at the old Douglass High School. Her friend Mr. Llewellyn Wilson taught music there and was the inspiration for Ethel's middle name. Thus from her earliest moments, music was a part of Ethel's life.

The Ennises left North Calhoun Street in 1936 and moved to 1208 Riggs Avenue. In September of that year, four-year-old Ethel started first grade at school number 111, located across the street from her house. There was a great fuss to make sure Ethel got off to a good start. Bell provided the notebook and pencils and Honey provided the asafetida bag. The latter was an old folk remedy, a matchbox-sized concoction worn around the neck on a string and used to ward off evil spirits. It worked, too: it smelled so evil that any evil spirit in its right mind would stay away.

Toward the end of first grade, Ethel first experienced having her picture in the paper. There at the back of the class sat little Ethel next to a chalkboard with bold white letters proclaiming, "IT WON'T BE LONG NOW." The message, of course, referred to those interminable last days of school in June. The words may have implanted themselves in young Ethel's mind. Later they would come to characterize the course of her career.

By the time she got to second grade, Ethel tried her hand (and voice) at performing. As she remembers it, "I was in a school play. I sang a spiritual, 'Swing Low, Sweet Chariot.' Instead of singin' the song straight, I raised my arm and pointed on 'Look over yonder.' For me this was bein' expressive 'cause I was kind of a 'mild child.' Maybe they knew I was gonna be a singer but I sure didn't."

"Mild child" though she may have been, by third grade her teacher, Mrs. Smith, a favorite, was sending home report cards with "comments." "She always put *'talkative'* on my report card. I don't know what the devil I was talking *about* 'cause I didn't have anything *to* talk about . . . I was probably just talking to *myself.*" This notion of Ethel's that she didn't have anything to talk about arose from that common child-rearing maxim that "children should be seen, but not heard." This was repeated so many times around the Ennis household that as Ethel grew up, she became firmly convinced that she had nothing worth talking *or* singing about.

Meanwhile, at home Ethel *did* have someone else to talk to after her baby brother Andrew arrived in March of 1938. Five-and-a-half-year-old Ethel was thrilled at her brother's arrival and immediately became his second mother, a role she still assumes today. If battles were to be fought and won on Andrew's behalf, Ethel took them on, but there was one thing that she had a hard time putting up with. "He started taking clarinet lessons when he was about seven years old, and it used to drive me *crazy.* I never could stand the sound of someone just learning to play the clar'net . . . the *squeaks* can really get on your nerves . . . ." Ethel's sensitive ears didn't have to suffer for too long, however. Andrew later switched to and mastered the tenor sax and eventually went on the road with Ray Charles for nine years before returning home to Baltimore.

As for Ethel's aversion to the clarinet, she was compelled to change her mind years later when she went on tour with the quintessential clarinetist of our time, Mr. Benny Goodman, "The King of Swing." There wasn't a squeak to be heard anywhere near Goodman's clarinet. Ethel had to admit, "You know, it's much better hearin' clarinet played by a man who knows his instrument."

Seven seemed to be the lucky year for starting music lessons. Just as Andy started clarinet at seven, Ethel was seven when she started taking piano lessons—but *not* because she *wanted* to. "I wanted to dance . . . to fly away . . . to express myself bodily. I wanted to be a ballerina." Today Ethel laughs as she conjures up the image of herself as a ballerina. "I mean, it was the thirties, and how many black ballerinas did they have back then? Mama did try to find me a suitable coach, but Honey opposed it. She said, 'Dancing is something you do "for the devil".' And Mama said, 'All the men teachers are "funny".' So that was the end of my career as a prima ballerina."

Just as Honey was the single most influential factor in Ethel's moral development, Bell was the driving force behind Ethel's musical growth. "Mama too was determined that I was going to be a lady—and *play the piano*. You had to cook, sew, and *play the piano*. I hated to take lessons. When other children were out playing and having fun, I had to be there practicing my scales."

In later years Bell made light of Ethel's struggle with piano lessons as she recalled, "Her uncle provided the piano and I provided the strap." Ethel saw it differently. Just as some pianists say that they studied under some*one*, Ethel says that she studied under some*thing*. Ethel calls it "parental domination," a term she learned early in life from Big Ethel Wise. And the *term* wasn't the only thing she learned about it—as always, experience was the best teacher.

When Ethel began to feel that her mother's will had been imposed upon her own desires, this seemingly perfect model of a child began to develop the heart of a rebel. However, as mentioned earlier, she didn't dare let it show, not knowing what evil fate would befall her if she did. She already knew that Honey had an ironing cord hanging on the wall, ready for whipping little girls who were "bad." Mama had passed on to young Ethel the story of how Honey had struck *her* when she had been a bad little girl. Mama's point made itself crystal clear in Ethel's mind. As Ethel recalls it, "Mama was sayin' Honey had an ironclad hand. Whenever Mama didn't do what Honey asked, she'd give her the back of the hand with a strong WHAP. Once Mama woke up under the table and didn't know how she got there. Anyhow, Honey would just let her lay there until she came to."

Ethel doesn't remember Honey being this way to Mama around her, but she did see what happened to Charlotte. One day Honey aimed a skillet at Charlotte when she accidentally forgot to put the "Ma'am" after the "Yes." Charlotte ended up with a bloody mouth and had to be rushed to the local doctor to have stitches sewn in her lip. Ethel knew that she didn't want these kinds of things to happen to her. It was simply easier for little Ethel to go along and obey; there was less fear in it. And *that's* how she went through the whole seven years of piano lessons. "I did it 'cause I was *told* to do it, not because I *wanted* to. I went whether or not I knew my lesson, just 'cause I said I would. I was not *involved*, that's for sure!"

Being *noninvolved* was the only way that young Ethel knew to get even. She did many things that way both during and after her childhood. It didn't hurt anyone else, but Ethel began to teach herself to protect her feelings by distancing herself from the pain—as well as the pleasure—of whatever the experience was. She was beginning to build a shell around herself. In addition she began to establish that central rule that most children do at some point, the one that says, "When I grow up, *nobody* is going to tell me what to do. I'm going to have *my* way, when I grow up." These early seeds took root and began to sprout later on in Ethel's career.

Back in those childhood days, Ethel, as "good" as she was, did manage to get punished from time to time. Once Bell gave her the strap for running out in the street during one of her fights on Andrew's behalf. Mind you, she didn't get whipped for fighting, but because she disobeyed and ran out in the street. Another time, Honey pulled out the ironing cord when Ethel and Charlotte accidentally set fire to the back porch while they were playing hairdresser and testing the wonders of the curling iron with some strands of hemp. Charlotte immediately made a fast getaway down the back stairs and around the block, while demure Ethel bravely stood up to her punishment. These were small warnings to remind Ethel of "who's boss around here."

Meanwhile, the piano lessons taught Ethel some other things about life as she rode the number 21 bus to her teacher's house. On the bus there were people whose skin was not the same color as her own. She also would see these people when she went shopping downtown with Mama. She saw that there were certain stores that these people could go into and she and Mama couldn't. And naturally she wanted to know why.

Most of Ethel's early life was lived totally in the black community. This was true when the family moved to the Gilmor projects when Ethel was nine, when she went to junior high at Booker T. Washington, and when she attended high school at the old Frederick Douglass. During most of Ethel's childhood, her life in the city stopped at North Avenue. Black people just weren't supposed to cross that line. Ethel had no desire to, but still, she had a few questions to ask.

"I used to ask Honey why I couldn't go in certain stores, theaters, or restaurants. She would tell me, 'Well, this is just the way things are set up for now. Accept it and one day God will reveal his plan. In the meantime, learn to understand and to be compassionate toward the white man.' Mama was bitter. She thought we deserved a better life. If she would see a white man who was a wino in the gutter, she would say, 'Look at that. There's a whole lotta white goin' to waste. He *has* the chances.'"

Honey's solution to the whole problem was her constant urging for her family to *achieve*. "She always told me that we needed to work on everything three times harder than the whites, just to be noticed. She said to be the best we could be at everything, to work harder, and to never be idle. And Honey *lived* what she said."

Ethel took Honey's words to heart and remembered them, that is, about most things. When it came to the piano lessons though, there was room for doubt. Almost against her will, Ethel learned to play the piano well. The fact is that whether young Ethel liked or disliked the lessons, they soon led to her first paying job when she was about thirteen years old: playing piano for the church Sunday school at fifty cents per week. This first gig was the beginning of her musical career thanks to Mama's "domination."

Parental domination extended to her days as a high school student at Douglass as well. "I would do my regular five-hour gig at school and have to come *straight home*. It was always, '*Come straight home!*' I couldn't belong to any choirs, any dramatic classes, nothing. I wanted to be a drum majorette. 'Never! No!'"

By 1946, when Ethel was a young teenager, the foundation for the rest of her life had been firmly established on all levels—spiritual, emotional, and musical. Honey's strong moral teachings along with Bell's unrelenting will on the issue of piano lessons, all in the context of the church, would serve as future sources of inspiration and confusion as Ethel traveled on her path toward stardom and the fulfillment of her life's plan. At this point in Ethel's life, there were some signs that she was musically gifted, and although she had put in her seven years at the piano begrudgingly, a year later at fifteen, it all began to pay off. The instrument that she didn't feel close to would ultimately lead her to discover the one that was her true gift and that she would feel very close to indeed—*her own voice.*

Ethel's father, Andrew Ennis, Sr., sixteen years older than his wife Bell, at first impressed her as a sophisticated, wealthy, "security blanket." Bell's bubble burst quickly once they were married. The Ennises lived in a modest apartment in a black ghetto on Baltimore's west side. When Ethel was born, three years after the Depression, times were lean.

Ethel was five when her baby brother Andrew was born. It was love at first sight. Their strong bond continues today.

Elizabeth Small, called Honey by family and friends, was Ethel's maternal grandmother. Iron-willed and God-fearing, Ethel adored and feared her at the same time *(right)*.

Honey's words of wisdom set four-year-old Ethel on the right path as she went off to first grade at School 111 in Baltimore. By June, Ethel received her first exposure in the local press *(below)*. Ethel is seated directly under the chalkboard with white bows in her hair. The message on the board, "It won't be long now," became one of Ethel's life long slogans.

The family's means were meager but Mama, with Honey's guidance, raised her children with the ultimate in grooming and propriety. Daddy left the child-rearing to the ladies. He was too busy earning a living as a barber to spend much time at home. Ethel was constantly admonished to be a lady. As she says, "If they told me, 'Don't'—I didn't. But if they told Andrew 'Don't'—he did it anyway."

By age eleven *(top)* Ethel was cooking Sunday dinner for the family while Mama played the organ and sang in the church choir. As she recalls, "Daddy always loved my cookin'."

In the photo below, twelve-year-old Ethel poses as an exotic princess for Halloween as a skeptical-looking buck peers over her shoulder. Ethel's love of costumes and exotic finery often expresses itself as part of her present day performances.

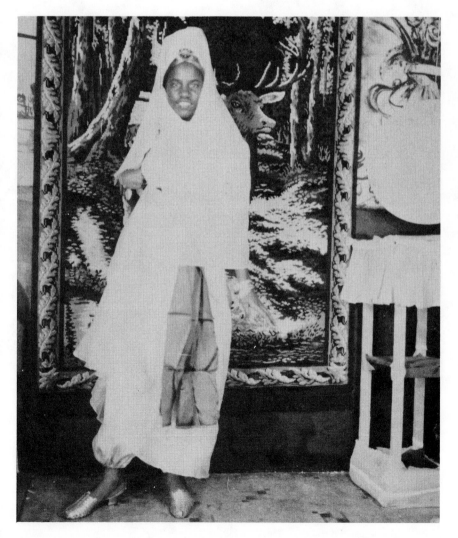

Shown here, Andrew and Ethel team up on a duet. While Ethel could barely tolerate Andrew's beginning squeaks and squawks on the "licorice stick," years later she had no complaints when she teamed up as singer with another clarinetist by the name of Benny Goodman.

In the Dark

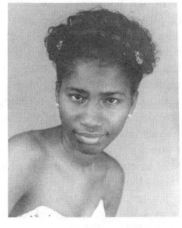

ST. JAHN STUDIO, BALTIMORE

*E*VEN though life for the black community in Baltimore was far different in the 1940s than it is today, one thing remains the same: teenagers, both black and white, *love* their music while the older generation often finds it difficult to tolerate. And so the battle goes on.

Back then, two dominant forces were present in the music world that would change the face of popular music forever. Mainstream white America was experiencing the first of three major pop explosions that have happened during contemporary times. In 1944, a skinny, blue-eyed kid from New Jersey who had a way with lyrics, phrasing, and a sense of romantic passion in his delivery created a scene of mass hysteria wherever he performed. His name was Frank Sinatra. At about the same time, black artists were producing their own unique sound. The instrumental ingredients of electric guitar and honking tenor sax, added to the soulful strains of blues and fiery excitement of gospel equaled a new genre, which came to be known as R&B (rhythm and blues). So while Sinatra fans were floating away on the strains of romantic ballads, teenagers in the black ghettos, who at that time were denied access to white theaters, clubs, and concert halls, were having their own good time jumping to the beat of R&B.

Like her contemporaries, Ethel Ennis heard the call of R&B, and like the others, she "dug" the beat. That old childhood longing to express herself bodily came back into the picture and right along with it came Honey's church-guided dogmas. Honey had already made it clear that "dancing was for the devil." So when Ethel discovered R&B, Honey came front and center to state her case. Ethel recalls, "Once she heard me playing this record by Dinah Washington and she said, 'That sinful record—what are you doing bringing that *common* music into this house?'" For Honey any music that wasn't church related, with the possible exception of classical, was considered vulgar and common. As for the blues, Honey regarded this type of music as totally self-demeaning. In her view the blues did nothing to inspire the human spirit; so once again she put her foot down. Listening to the blues was *strictly* forbidden, and Honey, as we have already seen, *meant business!*

Now a new problem arose. For Ethel the pull of the music was stronger than even Honey's heavy-handed admonitions. While she was still living in the projects, the notes of the blues would pulsate their way to her teenage ears through the cement floor of her living room from the apartment down below. Ethel's musical soul couldn't resist the temptation. So this ordinarily meek and always obedient child responded, against the wishes of her grandmother. There she was with her ear glued to the floor of the living room, trying to hear what was happening.

Ethel remembers it all very clearly. "I mean this lady lived down there, you know, the house with the red lights. And boy, you could smell the fried fish and the corn bread and hear the music. Boom! Boom! You could hear that bass line. Anyhow, havin' my ear down there and listenin' through that floor, that's how I learned a lot of things I wasn't supposed to learn."

In addition to secretly listening through the floor, Ethel openly bought and listened to a genre of recordings called "race records." "These were black singers who never got on the air. I used to buy their records like crazy. Some of the singers I used to listen to were Hadda Brooks, Camille Howard, Savannah Churchill, Rose Murphy, Laverne Baker. . . ."

There were others, too, whose scratchy, worn out records from the late forties and early fifties are still in Ethel's record collection. The styling, delivery, and selections of some of these female vocalists later influenced her own performance. There were tunes like "I'm Tired, Crying Over You" sung by Ella Johnson ("My mother used to sing it around the house."); "Fine Brown Frame" sung by Nellie Lutcher ("In the sixties I met Nellie. She told me she used to listen to me on the Arthur Godfrey Show. She said she thought I was an 'ofay' [white] chick."); and "Please Don't Freeze on Me" sung by Ruth Brown ("She was a rhythmic singer, very raw R&B. Her songs were sexy.").

"Mainly these were pop and R&B singers. I got to see them at the Royal Theater when I was in high school. They would work what we called 'the chittlin' circuit.' They might start at the Regal in Chicago, then to the Apollo in New York, the Earle in Philadelphia, the Royal in Baltimore, and then finish at the Howard in Washington, D.C."

While Ethel was strongly attracted to and loved listening to these female vocalists, the thought of seeing herself as a singer during those days was simply out of the question. "Once I did an audition for my piano teacher. I sang, 'Ah, sweet mystery of life at last I've found you...'." (Ethel imitates the flat shallow delivery of that first audition.) The piano teacher quickly made her assessment of Ethel's singing ability: "Nope! Forget it! You'll never sing!"

For Ethel at fifteen, life held no vision of a future filled with any kind of special excitement. In fact, if anything, it had settled into an ordinary kind of dull routine. She wasn't allowed to dance or listen to the blues, didn't want to continue the awful piano lessons, couldn't join in after school activities, and had no idea of doing anything with her voice. About the *only* thing left was to go along with Mama Bell's finishing school curriculum of sewing, cooking, and general housekeeping, and, of course, to maintain her decorum and be *a lady!*

But the muses had something else in mind the day Sylvester Coles, a classmate and neighbor, approached with some news. The all-male octet of which he was a member had an open chair for a piano player. He asked Ethel to consider filling the slot. This young jazz-playing group held rehearsals at Sylvester's house just across the street from the projects on Gilmor. Ethel didn't jump at the chance right away. First of all, she had her doubts as to whether or not she was capable of handling this kind of music (it was a far cry from the Sunday school repertoire she had been playing thus far), and secondly, she didn't know whether or not this was something she even *wanted* to do. One fact that didn't bother her at all was that she would be the only female member of an all-male group. At any rate, Ethel wanted to think about it for a week.

During the group's next rehearsal, Ethel decided to sit in, and there she met the group's leader, Abraham Riley. She discovered that most of the guys were not yet drinking age, so their gigs were restricted to relatively calm places like VFW and Fellowship Halls, as well as dances, mostly around the Randallstown area. Ethel felt comfortable enough with the idea and agreed that she would like to take on the job as the piano player for two dollars and fifty cents a week.

However, before she could give a full promise to the group, she had to secure Bell's permission. The group backed her all the way. Several of the older members of the band assured Mama that Ethel would be properly protected and delivered safely home after each gig. And the fact that rehearsals would be taking place right across the street, where Bell could keep watch on what was happening, convinced her that Ethel would be in safe hands.

As Ethel recounts, "Mama thought it would be OK 'cause at least we were inside rehearsing and not out on the streets. And of course she never had any idea that anything more would ever come out of it. She just looked at it for what it was—a group of young people who wanted to play music."

Ethel seemed to enjoy this new-found expression for her piano training, but Honey was right in there with her ever-present morality. She would see Ethel getting dressed to go out and play in what she referred to as "those beer gardens" and demanded to know, "Where's your undershirt, gal?" Ethel, who was fifteen and had graduated from this item of clothing, would exclaim with a bit of mild exasperation, "Honey, you don't wear an *undershirt* with a *strapless gown!*"

However, doing away with her undershirt and playing in "beer gardens" were minor violations. Next came the issue of not only *listening to,* but actually *playing* that "demeaning, common music" called *the blues.* It wasn't that Ethel had actually planned it that way, but it was bound to come up sooner or later. One night while the octet was playing a routine gig, someone in the audience challenged the group with an extra tip if someone could sing the words to an old blues number popularized by a singer named Lil Green. The title of the song was "In the Dark." Abraham Riley excitedly approached Ethel with the news and asked her if *she* just might happen to know the words to the song. Now, how "innocent" fifteen-year-old Ethel Ennis might have even remotely known the words to such a song, given all of those heavy-duty restrictions about listening to the blues, *still* remains a mystery to Ethel herself. The tune might have been one of those forbidden "common" music records she sneaked in when Bell and Honey were looking the other way. Or maybe the lady downstairs might have played it a couple of times. Regardless, those lyrics had found their way into Ethel's subconscious memory, where they were neatly stored away and ready to be pulled out for this very occasion. The guys in the band were delighted. The audience was thrilled. But nobody was more surprised with what happened that evening than Ethel herself.

" 'In the Dark' is one of those songs that's really gettin' down. I sang it and everybody applauded. Imagine that! My first time singin' and everybody applauded! And then when I finished, they asked me to sing it again and again. And I thought, 'Ooooh, I'm gonna be a singer *and* a piano player with this group . . . Maybe, I'll get paid doubly . . . Maybe I'll get *five dollars* a week instead of two fifty.' But that didn't happen. I still got only two dollars and fifty cents a week and now I was singin' my head off."

As it turned out, "In the Dark" became more than merely the title of the song that launched Ethel's singing career: it accurately represented Ethel's outlook during most of the time she spent in the business. Today Ethel unabashedly admits, "I didn't know what I was doing at the time. I just went along blindly and did it."

Meanwhile, back at home during those early gigs, Mama had her fair share of doubts and fears about what all of this activity eventually would do to her little girl. Sometimes she would go along and check it out for herself. Most of the time she would wait up until Ethel came home, which might be as late as 5 a.m. on nights when the band's van broke down. The order was, as it had been throughout the high school years, *"Come straight home!"* And straight home Ethel came. Eventually Bell convinced herself that the devil would not take over her baby's soul, and she surrendered to the idea that her daughter could work in those places and still "be a lady."

During the next year and a half, Ethel, still a high school student, continued to take on gigs with Riley's Octet. Throughout this period she began to evolve her skills as a vocalist and keyboardist. During those days, and even later on, the young singer never considered doing anything more with her craft than entertaining the immediate audience who happened to be around then and there. Unlike so many young musicians of today who are smitten with the idea of becoming a "star," Ethel claims that for her this was never the case. And while so many young musicians of today have a vast array of affordable recording technology at their fingertips, this wasn't true for Riley's Octet back in the late forties. Since tape recorders were not readily available, the group, if it wanted to experiment with sound, needed to set up a special recording session. And so when the inspiration hit, they set up a date with Henry O. Berman's recording studio down on Lombard Street where it stood until the very recent past.

One of the people who "hung out" with the octet was William Everhart, a young songwriter from Dundalk. Everhart came to the group with a selection of his creations and offered them for recording. The group chose two of these to cut on an acetate disc at Berman's studio. One of the tunes was a ballad entitled "Don't Ever Feel Blue" and the other was an up-tempo swing number called "Honey Please Hold Me Tight." While the group was delighted with the feedback from the disc, that was the end of it. They never intended to go commercial with the project, nor did they expect to create a hit.

However, Ethel and Everhart struck up a musical relationship, and their collaboration on a rock 'n roll number entitled "Little Boy" did go on to become a mild "hit." Savoy, a New York "sepia" label (this term replaced the earlier "race" designation as being less pejorative to black artists) picked up the tune, which they published and produced in 1950.

Eventually the song was recorded by no less than five nationally recognized artists, including the wildly energetic pioneer of rock 'n roll, Little Richard.

This initial foray into the realm of commercial music was the beginning of a long line of encounters that caused Ethel to question the sometimes murky ethics of the music industry. For while their song went on to become a success, the songwriters—not wise to the ways of "the biz"—never received any kind of financial remuneration.

Following closely on the heels of this experience, another I-wonder-what's-going-on-here situation occurred. This one involved some "monkeying around" with the machinery of a national talent competition. During Ethel's last year in high school, the music teacher, who recognized her talent, submitted her name as a contestant to a local talent show on Channel 13, then called WAAM. She handily won the competition with her rendition of "The Man I Love." This qualified her to go to Philadelphia to compete on "Paul Whiteman's Talent Show." Mama and Ethel excitedly boarded the train for Philadelphia and—who knew?—possibly even stardom. Those hopes were quickly dashed, however. Although Ethel had been rehearsing her winning song for several days before the final taping, right before she went on the air, she was suddenly confronted with the news that clearance couldn't be obtained for on-air performing rights. Ethel had to act quickly, so she pulled another tune out of her songbag, but this one did not fare too well for the young performer. She had barely rehearsed it and found it difficult to put her heart into a number called "My Mother's Eyes."

After her performance, she was informed that the applause meter was not registering accurately and that somebody was operating it manually with a string. Right then and there it should have been obvious to Ethel that in this very competitive business, there was a lot of "pulling of strings." But during those early days, Ethel didn't bother herself with learning the details of the bewildering business side of this complex industry. Her recurrent philosophy until very recently has been, "I didn't think I had to know anything about all that; all I ever wanted to do was sing."

So Mama and Ethel returned home from Philadelphia, perhaps a little wiser for the experience. Her defeat did not cause too much of an upset, however, for that very month, August, 1950, Ethel put out her shingle as a professional musician when she became a dues-paying member of the local union. And just in case her musical career didn't work out, she enrolled in Cortez W. Peters Business College the next month.

Ethel's life now began to take on a double identity. By day she was the earnest student plugging away at her shorthand and typing studies; at night she tickled the ivories and warbled her tunes at the Oasis ("The Worst Show in the World"), a strip club on "The Block," the city's infamous X-rated district. Honey raised her righteous eyebrow about *that*. In Grandma's view her ladylike granddaughter had now crossed the line from "beer garden" to "the devil's den" (which referred loosely to any environment that was not primarily church oriented). Actually the eighteen-year-old singer/pianist filled-in between acts while the girls were taking a breather. Like the lady Honey and Mama raised her to be, Ethel would disappear into another part of the building when she finished playing until it was time for her to go on again. By this time Ethel was discovering that there might be more to this music business than she had first imagined. As she later recalled, "Gee, you really learn life in a hurry working in places like that... You see so much and you're so amazed, you just say, 'Ooh, my goodness!'" Several months later, Ethel left the Oasis.

Honey breathed a sigh of relief; Ethel had passed the test. As far as this God-fearing grandmother was concerned, if her granddaughter could stand up to the "evil temptations" that were present in a place like the Oasis and come out unscathed, she could be trusted to work nearly anywhere.

However, right on the heels of the Oasis, the young singer innocently headed for the no-holds-barred, seamier side of the business. Her next gig was with another all-male group who played the night club circuit around town. The Tilters, as they called themselves, were a jumping, seven-member R&B ensemble, advertised by the white proprietors of one of the clubs as "The Nation's Hottest Sepia Band." Ethel accepted bookings with them as a single, playing piano and singing between the acts as she had done at the Oasis. But the Oasis was mild compared to the next round in "the devil's den." Some of the clubs where they played were fertile territory for explosive incidents. It didn't take much time before Ethel was a part of just such an outburst when the group was playing Sherrie's Musical Bar and Lounge on Pulaski Highway. Ethel has a lot to say about those days.

"Lots of truckers used to stop in there, and you know truckers. In those days, they were *kings*. Well, one of them called out, in an insulting fashion, 'Sing it, black girl' and that wasn't too cool. In those days we were called 'Negroes.' Well, The Tilters were upstairs on a break and got the word about this. Next thing, I remember seein' them come rushing down the stairs, and I mean, they were ready to *kill!* Then all I remember is seein' Arthur Nelson, the bassist, holdin' a gun and gettin' ready to shoot *up* the place... It took the rest of the guys to hold him down." (It wasn't surprising that Nelson became so concerned; it wasn't merely chivalry that got him so riled up—Ethel and he were "seeing" each other.)

A lot of the places where they took gigs in those fledgling days of Ethel's career were what she calls "raw places." (Substitute "joint" or "dive," it's all the same.)

"There was a difference between raw white places and raw black places. In the raw white places, there was a feeling like 'You're not wanted here, but entertain us.' We felt the anger of the whites, but we still played our music. Sometimes while I was playin', beer bottles would go zingin' by my ears. I'd be singin' and duckin' my head at the same time. Sometimes, mostly in black places, you'd see shootings and stabbings. And next thing you know, they're back at the bar. If blacks kill blacks, it's no big thing. If blacks kill whites, it's a big issue. And it's still that way. Juries are mostly white, so when a black kills a white, they do something about it."

About all of these wild and wooly goings-on, Ethel comments, "I just thought all of this was the way of the world . . . the way it was supposed to be. I mean, Honey warned me. She told me about 'the devil's den.'"

As if these events weren't dramatic enough, Ethel took on another self-appointed job with The Tilters. She became "the guardian of the light," except that in this case the light needed to be kept *off* in order to keep any would-be troublemakers "in the dark" about the interracial dating that was going on with two of the fellows in the band. "The girls would come to the club, but they couldn't be seen with the guys anywhere in the vicinity of the white communities. So we had to smuggle them out of the club and into the car. One of the guys had a '47 Dodge and when you opened the door, the light on the ceiling would stay on, so I had to keep my hand over the light so nobody would see the girls gettin' in. Then they had to stay down on the floor until we 'crossed the border' into a neighborhood where it would be safe enough for them to get up again."

In the midst of all this confusion, Ethel was more than keeping up with her studies at Cortez Peters. "I was going to school five days a week. I got out at three and worked two hours a day at the Health Department typing case histories. Then I would come home and get ready to work six hours at night at Gamby's on Pennsylvania Avenue with The Tilters. After two weeks of this routine I said, 'Later for this.' So I quit the Health Department."

Clearly Ethel had chosen the musical path above the secretarial one. But at her graduation in June, 1952, there was a brief moment of doubt. When the awards were presented, it was Ethel Ennis whose name was called for outstanding achievement in the area of shorthand. "When I got the award, I thought, 'Maybe I'm supposed to be a secretary instead of a singer.' But the thought didn't stay there for long. I'm glad I learned the shorthand though 'cause I use it all the time, even now, in writing down lyrics to my songs."

Meanwhile, Ethel continued to absorb her life-at-large curriculum, although the lessons were harder to take. By 1951 The Tilters had disbanded, and another group of five musicians, plus Ethel, formed a new group, the JoJo Jones Ensemble. With this group Ethel ventured farther afield and traveled on her first out-of-town gig to Providence, Rhode Island. She also confronted what it meant to be black and on-the-road during that time. "We would stop at some out-of-the-way diner to take out an order— just to get somethin' to eat. The people behind the counter didn't want to wait on us. If they did finally find it in their hearts to give us a glass of water, as soon as we finished drinkin' it, they would break the glass in front of our faces."

As harsh as this treatment was from the white world, it was small stuff compared to the way the members of the group dealt with each other. "After Rhode Island, we were booked into the Club Orleans on Orleans Street. JoJo, who was a little strange anyway, got bothered about something with the percussionist and pulled out his pen knife and stabbed him. It wasn't a deep cut, just a knick, but it was enough to draw blood."

A year later, not surprisingly, the JoJo Jones Ensemble split up. And then there were two: Ethel Ennis on piano and vocals and Montell Poulson on bass. Shortly after they started playing together, the duo took a job at the Dixie Hotel in Annapolis. Here there was a new lesson to learn. "The Dixie Hotel! That's where I met this black cat who told me he wanted to be my manager. He said he could introduce me to these people who had cut a recording. So he picked me up at home and Mama said everything was OK 'cause he could help me get ahead. Well, he took me to this place in Annapolis, and I thought, 'What's goin' on here? This doesn't look like an *office*; this looks like a place where people go to *sleep*.' And this one guy was movin' *out* and it looked like *we* were movin' *in*. This cat made advances and I know I had *murder* in my heart. I fought him. I kicked him. I told him I was sick. Oh God, I tried *everything*. Well, he finally backed off and apologized. He said he thought I was like the other entertainers he knew, but he found out I *wasn't*."

Fortunately these occupational hazards occurred rarely. Ethel's prime concern was with her music. She and Montell played at various night spots around Baltimore, places such as Phil's Lounge on North Mount Street and the Zanzibar on McKean and Baker. They also took on-the-road gigs as far north as Buffalo, New York. When they came back to town, they were booked into a club on Pennsylvania Avenue called the Club Casino. By this time the duo was beginning to groove. And the news was beginning to travel. It didn't have far to go to reach the ears of George Fox, who owned a club just a short distance up "The Avenue."

One night Fox and his wife Reba stopped by to check out this new up-and-coming singer. Whoever was spreading the word was, in the Foxes' opinion, right on target. They both fell in love with Ethel at first sight, but it was Reba who took one look and listen and declared excitedly, "*This* is a

Persian Room act!" (The Persian Room was once a plush showplace in the Plaza Hotel in New York City.)

At this point in 1954, Ethel had spent seven tough years learning her craft. At twenty-two Ethel had "honed her chops" and was ready to move into a spot that would be "home" for the next nine years. She had gained experience in life in general as well and had moved away, at least outwardly, from the sheltered upbringing of her earlier years. There was one thing, however, that Ethel carried with her from childhood, even in the heat of those "rough and raw" years, and that was her "good little girl" routine. There she was in the midst of chaos, and never once did it occur to her that her presence made any difference to what was happening around her. She merely wandered through these dramatic episodes in innocent, wide-eyed wonder. In Ethel's view, everything just seemed to *happen by chance*—including the appearance of the man who would become her first manager, George Fox.

III *Lullabys for Losers*

HE RED FOX—*red* because that was the color of Reba's hair and *Fox* for obvious reasons—was the name of the establishment on Pennsylvania and Fulton Avenues, an area that was neither black nor white. It was sort of a borderline, neutral, "everyman's" zone. In time, the names of Ethel Ennis and the Red Fox would be indelibly linked in Baltimore memories as part of the city's colorful past. Invariably, the mention of Ethel's name evokes a response such as, "Ethel Ennis—I used to hear her sing while I was in high school at that little club—what was its name? Oh yeah, the Red Fox."

During its heyday, from the mid-fifties to the late sixties, the Red Fox held a unique place as a night spot in the city. Here, liberals of all persuasions would gather—blacks, whites, scholars, priests, gays, straights—everyone loved the place! Music provided the common ground and kept the place "cookin'." The lineup of talented performers included vocalists Dolores Lynn and Irma Curry; pianists Lonnie Liston Smith, Claudie Hubbard, and Ray Chambers; vibraphonist Jimmy Wells; saxophonists Otts Lohn (alto) and Dave Hubbard (tenor); drummers Jimmy Johnson, Roland Thomas, Howard Kelly, and Bobby Nelson; bassists Irvin Turner,

Donald Bailey, Andy Rock, Phil Harris, and Montell Poulson; singles William "Earl" Omara (vocals and percussion) and Billy Foxx (piano and vocals).

Fox, a rotund, lovable, cigar-smoking New Yorker, loved the business, even though in a recent interview he claimed that he never made too much money on the place. In fact, the Foxes ran into a little snag with the IRS when they were new in the business and didn't realize that when they put in live music, they were required to pay an entertainment tax. Two years later they woke up with a start when the IRS presented them with a bill for $80,000 in back taxes.

One who remembers well the ups and downs of those early days at the Red Fox is Jimmy Wells, Baltimore's premiere vibraphonist. As Wells tells it, "Fox loved to go to the track and gamble on the horses. I could always tell when I walked in the door whether he won or lost that day. When he won, he would be all smiles and would greet me with a friendly, 'Good evening, how are you?' My vibes would be set up on the stand just like I left 'em the night before, ready for me to play. If he lost, when I came in, I'd see race track stubs all over the floor. Fox was nowhere around and my vibes would be upside down on the stand. I'd have to set 'em up all over again before I could go to work."

Even today, as Fox spends his days in sunny Florida retirement, his moods are still determined by the rise and fall of his fortunes at the track. George was always a gambler, a lovable "Guys and Dolls" character. He looked and acted the part to a tee—complete with his New York-Jewish manner of speaking, fat cigar, and pot belly. He found his way to Baltimore when the booking business that he ran in New York fell onto some hard times. As the story goes, he was (to put it delicately) run out of town. Then, too, Baltimore was home to his dear wife Reba and it was Reba who wanted to buy the carry-out liquor business on the corner of Pennsylvania and Fulton. So George went along and decided to open the lounge.

The room was opened by Lou Bennett, a talented organist who later moved to Europe and "made good." It was Bennett who led George and Reba to drop in on Ethel that first evening. Bennett was leaving Baltimore for a gig in Cleveland. Fox said, "Well, what are we going to do now? Who can we find to replace you?" Bennett replied, "Well, Ethel Ennis is playing at the Club Casino down 'The Avenue.' She'd be good for the room." The rest, as they say, is history.

As mentioned before, from the moment the Foxes heard Ethel sing, they were sold. Fox recalls, "I had hung out in night clubs all my life, especially around New York, so I knew something about the business. When I heard Ethel sing, I thought she was great. Her voice was so clear. Her diction was perfect. So I booked her into my place. In those early days when Ethel sang there, the room was beautiful. People used to come in and pay seventy cents for a drink and sit there all night listening and nursing down their one drink."

When Ethel started playing the club in 1955, her repertoire was comprised primarily of mellow ballads with a jazz flavor—such standards as: "Let There Be Love," "More Than You Know," "Smoke Gets In Your Eyes," "Lush Life," and "All About Ronnie." She also would sing "C'est Si Bon" and "Hey, Jacques," which she did in French ("My delivery could be more dramatic in French."), and her old high school favorite "Fine, Brown Frame." For fun, Ethel and Reba Fox would team up on "A Good Man is Hard to Find" (with their own variation on the lyrics). Ethel's top choice though was a beautiful Gershwin tune, "Love Walked In" ("I really thought I was *hot stuff* when I sang that tune.").

During those days the young vocalist would accompany herself on the piano, backed on bass by Poulson. Later other musicians were added. According to Fox, "Ethel was at her best during those early days. Later, when they gave her all that other jazzy stuff and she started moving around a lot, it wasn't like those early days." Several months after Ethel started playing the club, Adah K. Jenkins of the *Baltimore Afro-American* wrote in her column "Along The Avenue" (August 13, 1955):

> It appears that Ethel is on the threshold of stepping into a bright new world, thanks to the faith of George and Reba Fox, the two people who direct the fortunes of the club. . . .
> The groundwork has been laid for the velvet voiced Ethel to step into the big time and judging by her past performances at the RED FOX, she should be a solid success.
> [The Foxes] have spent time, money and effort in trying to advance her career, simply because they felt she deserved a big break and could become an outstanding star.

During the same time that the Foxes in Baltimore were busy laying groundwork for "velvet voiced" Ethel, a little farther south of the Mason-Dixon line, a manager of another up-and-coming singer was also laying his own groundwork. During the summer of 1955, this manager took several recordings released by Sam Phillips of Sun Records in Memphis, Tennessee to station WERE in Cleveland. The discs, which contained an unknown singer belting out a country song on one side and a blues on the other, were played on the air by DJ Bill Randle and immediately caused an explosive listener response. The electrifying young singer's name was Elvis Aaron Presley.

In Presley, Phillips found what he had been searching for. He once said, "If I could find a white man who had the Negro sound and Negro feel, I could make a billion dollars." In fact, in Memphis Elvis' recordings were first played by Dewey Phillips, a white DJ for station WHBQ.

Phillips' program, "Red, Hot, and Blue" was devoted to black blues artists. When he first played Elvis' recordings, the listeners were so convinced that Elvis was black that Phillips tried to dissuade him from making personal appearances. (Why blow a good thing?)

In their respective backgrounds, Elvis and Ethel shared some common experiences. Like Ethel, Elvis was a member of a family of devout church-goers. Presley's family attended the Assembly of God church, which was heavily Gospel oriented. When Elvis, like Ethel, discovered the hypnotic rhythms of R&B, he couldn't leave it alone. The reaction of the older generation in Memphis was the same as it had been in Baltimore. Down south, they called it "sinful music," but that didn't stop Elvis from heeding its call. Elvis' success in Cleveland led Colonel Tom Parker to negotiate a substantial contract with RCA Victor, the same label that Ethel would record with eventually—and that's where their commonality stopped. It wasn't in the stars for Ethel to create the spectacular sensation (and eventual tragedy) that was in store for Presley.

By 1956, shortly after Ethel's first album was released, Presley's "Heartbreak Hotel" launched the second pop explosion. Teenagers responded mightily and adopted new ways to dress, act, talk, and think—in short, they created a new culture born out of their angry expression of youthful conflict and rebellion. Thus in one bold stroke, two heretofore oppressed cultures found a voice through Presley—teenaged youths and southern blacks. The dynamics of this combination were staggering and would eventually shake the roots of the music industry, not to mention the very heart of our culture.

Ironically this entire movement was built on white southern teenagers trying to sing black, while the actual black artists who had inspired them stood a long way back in the shadows. The country simply wasn't ready yet to let go of its cultural biases, and the only acceptable way to get black music into the white mainstream was through white faces with black voices.

When Ethel began to record, the first wave of Sinatra's popularity had already crested, and although the momentum was still going strong, the musical genre that he and Ethel represented was heading for a period of comfortable stabilization. Following right in its wake, Presley's influence was gathering force and was about ready to break with an impact never before experienced in American pop music.

Where did Ethel Ennis, a shy, black, jazz-oriented ballad singer fit into these shifting musical tides? Perhaps if George Fox had been aware of what was about to happen, he never would have devoted himself to building Ethel's career, and it all would have stopped for Ethel right there at Fulton and Pennsylvania Avenues. But George Fox was a gambler. With Ethel, Fox found a new filly on which to place his bets. He and Ethel talked it over, and he became not only Ethel's first manager, but her "great white father" as well. Fox would be the first of many "white fathers" (and mothers, sisters, and brothers) who would open doors that otherwise would have been closed to a black, female singer at that time.

Early in her days with Fox, the doors began to open—and not always for the better. On this particular occasion, the doors were in New York City, but the script was another variation of the same theme that Ethel had earlier encountered at the Dixie Hotel in Annapolis. Fox, in his new capacity as Ethel's manager, now had a valid reason to return to the hustle and excitement of his native city. He booked Ethel into a club called the Beau Brummel, named for the nineteenth-century British figure of elegant fashion. The club catered to the fashion industry and it wasn't long before one of the "big names" in that world spotted Ethel and made his move.

"There I was on stage doin' my gig and this guy comes right up and says to me, 'Five hundred dollars—go to bed!' I got really befuddled. There I am tryin' to *sing* and he wants me to *swing*. Some people don't know the difference between an *evening* gown and a *night* gown! So I tried to get rid of him and sent him over to Fox, who told him, 'She doesn't *have* a price tag.' And then the cat got really angry and answered, '*Everybody* has a price tag.' Fox just sneered at him and said, 'Well, here's *one* who doesn't.'"

These advances were no doubt connected with some mysterious myth about the lifestyle of being an entertainer. From the beginning Ethel's upbringing allowed no place for these kinds of shenanigans. And from the beginning Ethel was out to prove that "*Ladies* can sing and be *in* that world, but not *of* it." To Ethel, the life of an entertainer looked "self-denigrating," a world that "would eat you up alive and use you up instead of leading to fulfillment." This attitude still prevails: "I never wanted the life of an entertainer. I just wanted to be a person who sings. I never wanted to look like what people *think* an entertainer *should* look like. You know, with leopard coats, furs, big earrings, lots of jewelry, and heavy make-up. I don't mind *style*, but I like a *well-groomed* look. From the beginning, I never wanted to be a myth or my 'act' all the time; I just wanted to be a real person. That was the *only* way I could stay in the business."

When Ethel started at the Red Fox, she was shy, withdrawn, and aloof, definitely the opposite of the engaging, buoyant, and warm personality that she projects today. If others had doubts, George's answer was, "Ethel has to grow on you." So while Ethel was slowly growing on people in his club, George set the wheels in motion to secure a recording contract.

On the home front, life at the Ennis household was in a state of transition. "Mama and Daddy had decided to separate. We moved out of the projects when I was twenty-three. Andrew and I moved with Mama to

Whittier Avenue. We were really on our own now and it was my first experience in feeling responsible for the family. I would help with the rent, even more than I had been doing before, and with Andrew, who was still in high school, and with taking care of the house. While Mama was at work, I would listen to my music, or work on drawing or cooking. Honey always said, 'Never be idle,' so I always found things to do to develop myself." During this same time, Ethel also began a two-year courtship with Jacques "Jack" Leeds, a young attorney whom she met during an intermission at The Red Fox.

For Ethel life was becoming very full. There really wasn't much time for socializing since nights were filled with singing, days with household chores, and, in between, with seeing Jack whenever she could. Ethel's gig started at nine but she admits, "I was always late. I was supposed to go on at nine, and I would just be comin' in the door." After work seemed to be the best time to "meet and eat," so some of the musicians and fans would find their way to McCulloh's Delicatessen for potato salad, wings, and greens, or to Jimmy's on Fulton Avenue, "the chittlin' place." These were black eateries, but in later years when life became more openly integrated, they would frequent The Plaza on Pennsylvania Avenue and Nate's and Leon's on North Avenue.

By November of 1955, Fox had negotiated and signed a deal with Jubilee, a small, nationally distributed record label. Ethel was delighted with the possibility and delivered the news to Mama. "Mama was excited. She thought it was terrific. Her little girl *doing* something . . . she liked that. Mama went up with me to the recording session in New York. During the whole session, she just sat there crocheting, but I could tell, she was really excited."

Fox paid the production costs, which amounted to $648 at that time. The entire album and a single were done in one session that lasted about three to four hours. The album contained ten cuts, a compromise between what Ethel wanted to sing and songs on file at Jubilee. Some of Ethel's choices were "Blue Prelude," "Offshore," and "Hey Jacques."

The young vocalist was bitten by the production bug instantly. Above all, she was impressed with the musicians. "I practiced my stuff in Baltimore and the producer got the musicians. They were pros all the way: Hank Jones on piano, Eddie Biggs on guitar, Abie Baker on bass, and Kenny Clark on drums. Their musicianship was so great that we didn't even need a rehearsal, just a quick rundown of the tunes. I didn't have to worry about the piano either, so I was free to just sing—and with perfect backing."

As good as that first studio looked to Ethel then, recording studios were almost "primitive" back in the 50s compared with later post-rock, multitrack technology. That first album was cut on one-track mono, so there was little room for error without a lot of tedious "cutting and pasting." Yet in many ways this first attempt was the most pure and unspoiled of all of Ethel's recordings. In its very simplicity, this album captured an integrity of style that later, high-tech productions seemed to lose.

The album cover features a head shot of a baby-faced Ethel Ennis looking much younger than her twenty-three years. The liner notes predict: "From the reactions of the Jazz Cognoscenti who heard the playback on this session, Ethel Ennis will make it." The press release agreed: "Both [the album and the single] were instantaneous successes judging from the excited DJ reaction around the country. Many stars are made but in this case one was born."

It appeared as if the machinery had been set in motion for a sure win. But that first album carried a prophetic title, *Lullabys for Losers*, and for George Fox, as the investor, that's exactly what it was. Once again the "hanky panky" in the business was at work. The album was selling, but statements from Jubilee bore no such evidence. Fox requested an adjustment, but none was forthcoming. Next, he tried an attorney, without success. Using another tack, he made a deal with a promoter to move the single "Offshore" backed with "I've Got You Under My Skin." Instead of promoting the record, the man made some tapes and "bootlegged" the copies. There seemed to be nowhere to turn.

Throughout the years, *Lullabys for Losers* has been licensed by various labels and reissued under several titles, most recently in 1977 by Nippon/Columbia in Japan. As for Ethel and Fox cashing in on any of this action, it was a lost cause; just one more piece of evidence to feed Ethel's growing skepticism towards the recording industry.

However, on the flip side of the record, so to speak, *Lullabys for Losers* was a winner for Ethel Ennis, the budding artist. DJs were beginning to play it on the air. In Baltimore, when a young jazz afficionado first heard one of the cuts on station WITH, he excitedly called DJ Roz Ford and asked, "What was the name of Sarah's [Vaughan] new release that you just played?" Ford replied, "That wasn't Sarah, it was a local girl. She's right here in town at the Red Fox. Her name is Ethel Ennis."

Shery Baker hightailed it over to the Red Fox as soon as he could and instantly became an ardent Ennis "evangelist." He began showing up at the club with an evergrowing stream of "converts." Roz Ford also checked in occasionally. On one of these evenings, Baker buttonholed Ford and requested that he give more air-play to Ethel's album. Ford agreed—on the condition that requests be sent to the station. "OK," Baker thought, "I'll play his silly little game." So he marshaled his growing forces and enlisted them in filling out a hundred post cards that he sent to the station.

Weeks later the album still wasn't being aired enough to suit Baker. The next time Ford appeared at the club, Baker, who by now had developed a strong case of righteous indignation, went right for his jugular with a few well-chosen barbs. Ford felt that his DJ status warranted, at the very least, preferential treatment. He didn't have to be *treated* this way. So he turned on his heel and fled huffily out the door, threatening never to return again.

Fox calmed down Baker and pleaded with him to apologize. After all, this wasn't good for business. Eventually, Baker cooled off enough to write a letter to Ford admitting that his manner was a bit brusque, but he never forgave him for not upholding his end of the bargain. Meanwhile, behind the piano, while heated tempers flared, innocent Ethel sang her dreamy ballads, blissfully unaware.

While DJs were spinning the cuts on the air, Fox connected with an agency who booked Ethel as a single into supper clubs and jazz rooms up and down the East Coast. Some of the clubs were elegant white rooms; others were black jazz clubs. As Ethel moved back and forth across the color line, she seemed able to please them all.

However, the true test for any black performer during that period was the Apollo Theater in Harlem. This temple of black music was the beginning and the end of the "chittlin' circuit." In its day from 1934 through 1976, it had the flavor of a music hall, vaudeville show, and Gospel church all rolled into one. Audiences here were known to be tough, and sometimes a poor unfortunate who wasn't up to par would be pulled off stage by a long stick hooked around his neck. Happily, this get-the-hook routine was reserved only for the Wednesday night amateur show. Those who were booked into the Apollo for a regular gig called it "the workhouse." They generally performed five shows a day, seven days a week. As Ethel says, "You met yourself comin' off the stage."

Virtually all of the greats had gone through rites of passage at the Apollo—Billie Holiday, Sarah Vaughan, Ella Fitzgerald, and, in 1956, Ethel Ennis. She remembers it vividly: "The owner of the Apollo, Frank Schiffman, really knew his audience well and he didn't want to see his performers die out there on the stage. When I started the gig, I opened with a cool jazz number. It got a so-so response. Schiffman stepped in and suggested that I open with a hot R&B number called 'You Gotta Drive, Daddy, Drive.' He knew what he was talkin' about 'cause that one they really dug!"

Ethel never had to worry, though; she always had the security of her "home base" in Baltimore at the Red Fox. She tied the knot to the city tighter still when she married Jack Leeds in 1957. By this time the ambitious young attorney was doing well in his thriving law practice and went on to become a city solicitor in 1959. A year later he was chosen to serve as an assistant attorney general, a high ranking position in the state for a black man at that time.

The future seemed to shine brightly on the couple as they settled in at their apartment on Druid Hill Avenue. Not long after, Shery Baker, who had a penchant for befriending entertainers, went to New York to visit another singer-friend of his. He took along Ethel's album. Some time in the predawn hours, after the clubs had closed, Shery and his friend were into some serious partying. He played the album. At first she didn't pay it much mind, but as the sounds continued to spin their magic into the air, Ethel grew on her. "Who is this bitch from Baltimore?" she wanted to know. "She has the great voice." With this pronouncement Baker put a call through to Ethel. Ethel fumbled around getting to the phone, heard who the speaker said she was, thought it was some prank, and handed the phone to Jack. Jack was convinced it was no prank and put Ethel back on the phone. That settled, the person on the other end of the line intoned in her unmistakable voice, "You're a musician's musician. You don't fake. Keep on singing that way . . . one day you'll be famous." Although Ethel was too sleepy and stunned to know it then, with that phone call, the torch had been passed. The speaker was Billie Holiday. A few years later, she would be dead.

Meanwhile, George Fox struck up another record deal, this time with ATCO, a subsidiary of Atlantic, a bigger label than the earlier Jubilee. This time they simply cut a single, a 45 rpm. The disc's title, which never went down in music history, was "Pair of Fools" backed with "Got It In My Blood to Love You." Ethel herself barely remembers anything about it except for the fact that this was the first time she overdubbed her own voice and that the arranger for the session was Ray Ellis, who was one of the last of that breed to work with Billie Holiday.

Oddly enough, even though Ethel knew of the legendary stature of Lady Day, had been touched by her personally, and now had worked with her arranger, she had never taken the time to really listen to Billie. Shortly before the great lady died in 1959, Ethel finally took the time, largely due to Shery Baker's dogged persistence. As Ethel puts it, "I went to Billie Holiday school with Shery. He was the one who taught me about Billie. It was Billie this and Billie that. Everything was Billie, Billie, Billie."

Just as Shery had tucked Ethel's album under his arm to play for Billie, he now tucked Billie's album under his arm for Ethel to play. The album was *Lady in Satin*, one of her last. The arranger was Ray Ellis. The experience of listening to Billie, really *listening*, is still vivid and clear for Ethel.

"I was in the apartment on Druid Hill Avenue by myself. It was at night and I turned out all of the lights and just listened. I closed my eyes to be with Billie's essence and suddenly it became very clear and bright. I got her deep emotion, her poetry. She painted pictures like Mabel Mercer when she sang, and she had the sound of a horn player.

"I began to understand that having a pretty voice is just icing. It's what you do with what you have that counts. I saw that you have to con-

jure up your whole being into your song—that's when it's felt and understood 'cause then it's the truth. And you have to go deep, very deep if you
want to be heard.

"I kept all of this in mind and worked with it, but it took me years to
really know this. I didn't know it until I lived life as much as I could.
Listenin' to Billie, that's when I became aware of singin' songs that I could
relate to and tell. It's more meaningful than just singin' a song just to sing.
She taught me to sing songs that I've experienced, songs that I've lived.
That's the only way you make 'em come alive.

"Billie was diggin' from whatever she had left. It was like a cry, as if
she was sayin', 'This is what I want to leave here.'"

The urgency and total dedication to her art that Ethel sensed in Billie
was not a feeling that she shared until quite recently. While it was true
that Ethel loved to sing, she never viewed it as a career—never. On this
point Ethel is adamant: "I just liked to sing. I never wanted to be a star.
To me it was like a hobby that I happened to get paid for."

Others like George Fox, fellow musicians, loyal fans, booking agents,
and record producers didn't see it that way. By the end of Ethel's first
decade in the business, all signs seemed to point to some future fame and
greatness. True, she didn't cause the stir that Elvis did—she simply wasn't
that kind of singer—and that, among other factors, may have had a lot to do
with how Ethel's career eventually unfolded.

Nonetheless, by November, 1957, when Ethel reached the quarter
century mark in her life, one thing was obvious—she had a tremendous
amount of promise as a vocalist. Billie Holiday wouldn't be the last "great"
to notice this; just around the bend, Benny Goodman was looking for someone just like Ethel Ennis.

IV   Change of Scenery

T HE KING OF SWING—that's what they called him. The title
was first bestowed upon Benny Goodman on August 21, 1935, when
his big band brought down the house at the Palomar Ballroom in
Los Angeles. As always in such matters, there were those who felt that this
accolade never rightfully belonged to Benny Goodman. What about Duke
Ellington or Count Basie? And what about Fletcher Henderson, who had
his own big band and whose arrangements Goodman had used to set the
crowd off on that historic evening?

Goodman's story goes back even earlier than Presley's, but it was the
same "schtick." Here again, swing, originally a black musical phenomenon,
was adopted by the whites and it was they, not the blacks, who got the
public acclaim. Remember the Duke's "It Don't Mean a Thing If It Ain't
Got Swing?" He wrote and popularized it in 1932, three years before
Goodman's ascent to the throne.

Assuredly, Goodman was not out to take something that wasn't his.
He had a lot of respect and admiration for talented black musicians and
used his success to break through the color barrier that existed then.
Goodman became the first band leader to use integrated bands at a time

29

when this was an unheard of practice. For a musician as great as Goodman, good musicians were good musicians—red, white, black, or yellow didn't matter—what counted was the color and quality of their music.

Swing demanded not only good musicians, but *lots* of them. A classic big band configuration usually included a rhythm section (piano, bass, drums, guitar), a reed section (saxes, clarinets, flutes), a brass section (trumpets and trombones), sometimes strings, and a male and female vocalist. The sound was lush, smooth, danceable, and obviously expensive to produce and maintain.

By 1945, at the end of World War II, the short-lived swing era was over. The post-war economy could no longer kow-tow to such luxuries. Sadly for jazz lovers, those nine years of swing were the only period in American history that any form of jazz ever appealed massively to popular taste.

When swing was on the decline in the US, Goodman established his popularity abroad and had many successful European tours. Along the way he made many friends, not only for his music, but for America as well. So it was only fitting that he was awarded yet another title, Ambassador with a Clarinet. This time even the diehards were hard pressed to question the honor.

It was in this latter capacity that Goodman was busy with preparations in March, 1958. He was piecing together his band and repertoire for a musical assault on the World's Fair in Brussels, Belgium. The American Pavilion needed it: our poor cultural showing was made doubly embarrassing by the presence of the Russian Theater, staring at us right across the way. No doubt we would have finished the Fair with cultural egg on our face had not Westinghouse Broadcasting Corporation stepped in to save the day.

Several months prior to the Fair's opening, Westinghouse received word that the American Performing Arts project at the Fair needed a financial shot in the arm to liven up its offerings. Reports from the Fair confirmed this view. The lavish American Theater opened with the movie "South Pacific," which produced little more than a yawn from foreign audiences. And to make matters worse, the competition for attention among the represented nations was, as one reporter put it, "savage." Thus it was fortunate that Westinghouse stepped in and shelled out $100,000 as a public service contribution to the State Department to send over what they considered to be our best cultural export—American jazz. Any why not, WBC reasoned, send a man who had a proven track record? So they chose Benny Goodman.

While all this was happening, Ethel was busily warbling away in the Capitol recording studios in New York City. George Fox had finally done it! In his unending quest for the perfect record deal, he seemed to have hit it lucky with Capitol Records in late 1957. This time Ethel was in league with some hot company. Other Capitol songstresses recording on the label in the late 50s included Peggy Lee, Dakota Staton, Keely Smith, and June Christy.

One of those who was largely responsible for Ethel's performances on Capitol was producer Andy Wiswell. As he remembers it: "I first met Ethel when she brought me an audition record while I was at Capitol. I signed her, as I was greatly impressed with [her] ability to sing ballads and up-tempo tunes with a wonderful feeling for vocal command." Wiswell's background was with big bands, lush orchestral arrangements, and Broadway shows, none of which had any connection with Ethel's musical roots. However, nobody in the recording industry asked Ethel about her preferences: she was simply assigned her songs and did what Wiswell told her to do.

Ethel eventually cut two LPs for Capitol Records. In the midst of recording one of these, *Change of Scenery,* she was heard by Popsie Randolph, the photographer who was shooting the publicity shots for the back of the album. Randolph had been a drummer with Goodman's organization at one time and was thus privy to a hot lead, one that could result in a big change of scenery for Ethel in more than name only. "Look," he told her, "Benny is looking for a new female vocalist to sign up for his 1958 European tour. They're going to end up at the Brussels World's Fair. I think you could fill the bill. Why don't you go over and audition?"

"Maybe," Ethel thought, "I *could* be the one to fill the bill." At the same time, the rumor was that anywhere from eighty to eight hundred young ladies were also trying to fill the bill. In an uncharacteristic display of ambition and courage, Ethel took the chance.

"At first I thought Goodman might be difficult to get in and see. And I remembered my childhood thoughts about squeaky clarinets. But somethin' told me I'd better check this one out."

Fox, usually in attendance and especially in New York City, went along with Ethel to Goodman's office while she auditioned. "I played the piano and sang; I think it was 'I'll Take Romance.' All Benny Goodman did was smile. He doesn't say too much, he's a man of few words. When I finished, it was like 'Don't call me, I'll call you.' So I went back to completing my recording session and went home to Baltimore."

At this point it was mid-March, 1958. One day at the end of the month, Fox came barging jubilantly into the club. Lady luck had done it: his filly had won by a long shot. George Fox beamed as he delivered the news to Ethel: "I've got a telegram for you to report for rehearsal for the European tour." Ethel was stunned. "There I was in this little night club in Baltimore and suddenly I was going to the Brussels World's Fair with one of the greatest bands in the country."

Word of this stroke of good fortune traveled around the city with lightning speed. Ethel's victory became a cause of jubilation for all of those around her—her husband, family, fans, musicians, as well as the entire city of Baltimore. *Sunpapers* reporter Patrick Skeane Catling in his column of March 26, 1958, spoke eloquent words of praise:

> To speak of Ethel Ennis in terms of the known, one must call her a second Ella Fitzgerald, with hints of Sarah Vaughan and Peggy Lee. These are her favorite singers and all of them, especially Ella Fitzgerald, have influenced her style, which is robust, fluent, sweet and hot.
>
> But she's not an unimaginative imitator. She's not merely a second Ella Fitzgerald. She's the first Ethel Ennis.
>
> Benny Goodman, in his quiet, restrained way, is crazy about her. He has signed her up for an extensive European tour to precede the climactic cultural assault on Brussels.

Above all, Ethel's good news was most deeply felt and shared by her own people, not only locally, but nationally as well. *Ebony*, the *Life* magazine of the black world, ran a major spread on Ethel's success in their June, 1958, issue. The photo essay captured the whirlwind of activity that preceded her departure for Brussels: rehearsals with Goodman, Ethel and fans at the Red Fox, shopping forays for her on-tour wardrobe (Benny requested something not too frilly and with a young, fresh look), and loving moments with brother Andrew, Daddy, and husband Jack.

The black community had reason to be proud: Ethel was another example of one of their own making it. They needed as many of these moments as they could get. By the late fifties the racial climate in the United States was "all shook up," not only with Presley's song by that name, but by a series of legal and grass roots attempts to gain equal rights for blacks. In 1954 the Supreme Court ruled racial segregation in public schools to be unconstitutional. Several months later the same decision was reached regarding bus segregation as a result of the Rosa Parks incident in Montgomery, Alabama. Apparently these moves were too much for the white Southern tradition to handle. On March 12, 1956, one hundred one Southern congressmen called for massive resistance to the Supreme Court desegregation ruling. But the law stood. In 1957 the power of the law was challenged again in Little Rock by Arkansas Governor Orval Faubus when nine black students were barred from entering Central High School. President Eisenhower would have none of it and sent federal troops to the site to enforce the court's order.

At the same time, the counter-culture found a new hero in Jack Kerouac, whose beatnik bible, *On the Road,* was being gobbled up by intellectuals across the country. Democracy and freedom were being tested all over the place in all kinds of ways. And Ethel Ennis had been selected as one of those to represent this great culture overseas. During this critical time, Benny's mission was important for our nation. Clearly it was as much a matter of diplomacy as it was of music. Of course, as always, none of this was Ethel's concern. She was simply going along to do her gig.

And what a gig it was! Goodman assembled the best musicians he could find to fill his eighteen-member band (including Goodman himself on clarinet). Vocalists were selected with the same ear for perfection. The male voice was provided by a legendary figure in his own right, Mr. Jimmy Rushing, one of the great blues singers of all time, who spent the first fifteen years of his career with the Count Basie Band. He became known as "Mr. Five by Five," not only because of his size, but for the tune he popularized by the same name. The female voice was provided by Miss Baltimore-meets-Brussels, Goodman's velvet-voiced ingenue, Miss Ethel Ennis.

After a month of intensive rehearsals, they gathered up all of their horns, drums, guitars, basses, and clarinets, their wardrobes, energy, and fortitude and headed for the airport on Saturday, May 3, bound for Stockholm, Sweden. To keep things running smoothly for the organization, road manager Jay Feingold and Benny Goodman's executive assistant Muriel Zuckerman joined the company. The members of the group needed someone to keep their heads straight: their superblitz itinerary covered sixteen cities in eight countries in a four-week period.

Meanwhile a crew had been sent ahead by Westinghouse to prepare for production of a fifty-five-minute film to be aired back home at a later date. Arrangements were also underway to broadcast several concerts into millions of homes in Belgium, France, Italy, and England through Eurovision, a television cooperative that joined forces for special events such as this. Voice of America was also on hand to send one of the concerts all over Europe and the Orient. Back home hundreds of American radio stations stood ready to pick up the swinging sounds from Brussels. This was a cultural event of immense magnitude, so it was no wonder that the press and media were climbing all over each other to cover it.

Before the band descended on Brussels, however, they spent three weeks warming up and thrilling audiences all over Europe. As they touched down in Stockholm on Sunday, May 4, the red carpet was waiting. They were greeted with cheers, champagne receptions, parades, and an outpouring of love wherever they went. It's a known fact that Europeans (and now the Japanese) have always responded to American jazz with more fervor than we ever did at home. Ethel says it's because ". . . in jazz there is freedom. You can say what you want to say at that moment. Americans are known for freedom, and jazz is one idiom where you can be free and it's accepted."

During their first week they performed in Stockholm, Sweden; Copenhagen, Denmark; Oslo, Norway; Hamburg, Germany; and ended the week with a spectacular concert in Berlin. At Deutschland Halle they performed in an arena packed with 12,000 Germans who gave them a rousing standing ovation. Ethel was overwhelmed. Never had she sung in front of so many people at one time.

The All-Stars, as they were called, began week two with a Sunday concert in Frankfurt and then flew down to Zurich for two days of concerts there. On Wednesday morning they boarded a train that carried them through the grandeur of the Swiss Alps as they headed for an evening concert in Amsterdam. From there they wended their way to the little Dutch village of Blokker.

"I remember Blokker," Ethel recalls, "That's where we were part of a parade. We were riding in a motorcade headed toward a warehouse that had been converted to a concert hall for our performance. I can still see the villagers lined up on both sides of the road—waving, pointing, and shouting, 'Ooh, ooh, look at the niggers.' But they didn't mean anything by it; they were just so surprised at seein' somethin' that looked strange to them. They loved Benny Goodman, so they loved anyone who performed with him. In Blokker, like everywhere else we went, there were always full houses."

They finished out the week in Germany with concerts in Cologne and Munich.

To kick off week three, the group had the Austrians clapping their hands and stamping their feet as they performed a double concert at the Konzerthaus in Vienna. Then it was back into Germany once more to perform in Essen, Stuttgart, and Hannover.

On Sunday, May 25, the band arrived at their ultimate destination— The American Theater, Fairgrounds, Brussels World's Fair. There they were happily greeted by relieved US officials—and seven days of rain.

Fortunately, most of the concerts were indoors and the rain didn't in the least quench the spirit of the jazz-loving fans who came to hear Goodman. Earlier in the day, even before the band arrived, the message at the box office was "Sold Out Tonight" in three languages: English, French, and Flemish.

The opening concert that Sunday evening started the wire services clicking. The word went out from Brussels to New York, 3,668 miles away, that Goodman and his musicians had gloriously accomplished their mission for America. Not only did the American papers echo the thunderous applause that Benny's triumphant performance elicited, the foreign press, too, was wildly impressed. *Le Soir, Le Peuple, La Derniere Heure,* and *Laatste Nieuws* all gave their stamp of approval to American jazz. The Detroit *Times* summed it all up: "Benny Goodman has scored a triumph at the Brussels World's Fair . . . US prestige rode high again on the clean, throbbing notes of a musical expression that is authentically and uniquely American. . . ."

And how did Ethel Ennis, America's talented, black, female representative feel about all of this at the time? Looking back on the tour, Ethel says, "I didn't understand the significance of everything that was going on. Had I understood the greatness of it all, I probably would've been scared. This way I was just doing what comes naturally."

Doing what comes naturally sometimes involved a little improvisation on Ethel's part, as evidenced by comments from *Herald Tribune* syndicated columnist John Crosby. As he reported from Brussels: "Mr. Goodman's new and splendid band sounded great, but . . . a new and talented girl named Ethel Ennis could be heard only intermittently. . . ." The column goes on to say that theater officials claimed this was because Columbia was recording the concert for the *Benny in Brussels* album and had toned down the theater to eliminate feedback. On the other hand the Westinghouse people heatedly denied this and claimed that the public address system wasn't very good and that they had to go out and replace it the next day.

Years later when Benny was appearing in Baltimore, Ethel had a little confession to make. "I told him, 'There was one song you didn't call up during the whole tour, "My Old Flame." One day you called it up and I had forgotten the words to the verse. I didn't know what I was going to do, but I had to think up something in a hurry so I just stood in front of the mike and mouthed some words during the parts I didn't know. Of course, nobody could hear anything 'cause I wasn't singin' anything. All the technicians started runnin' around pullin' plugs and stuff, thinking we were havin' technical difficulty. They couldn't figure out what went wrong. And then when it got to the part that I remembered, I just burst out singin' and everybody could hear again. The technicians were really relieved.' "

Goodman didn't remember any of this. Ethel says that he was still a man of few words, but with a wonderful smile. He was glad to see that she was well and still singing.

On the other hand what Benny probably *did* remember was his Belgian birthday celebration. On their last Saturday night in Brussels, the rain finally stopped, and the concert moved outdoors to the medieval town square in downtown Brussels. Here at the Grand Place, amidst seventeenth-century guild halls, etched in gold and built atop cobblestones, the Belgians presented Benny with a birthday party that was a happening. Richard Pack, author of the liner notes on Benny's album, states: ". . . the

Belgians staged a costumed spectacle of Flemish folk dancers, flag wavers, and stilt walkers in curious but charming counterpoint to the jazz concert. At one point, the traditional Flemish stilt walkers on their ten-foot stilts stomped around the square to the beat of 'Let's Dance.' Quite a sight!"

Some of the excitement of the Brussels concerts was preserved for all time on the previously mentioned *Benny in Brussels* albums (there are two volumes) produced by Columbia Records. What an opportunity for Ethel, right? Wrong! Here again this venture turned out to have another one of those weird twists that always seemed to be hovering around Ethel and her recording deals. Although everyone else in Benny's band, including Jimmy Rushing, was represented on the album, there was absolutely no sign of Ethel Ennis; not even the mention of her name. What could have resulted in a major recording breakthrough for Ethel instead ended up getting lost somewhere in the mists of time (and possibly in a vault at Columbia studios.) Ethel's label (Capitol) and Goodman's label (Columbia) did not strike a deal that would have released Ethel to record on Columbia. Furthermore, Capitol failed to use the Goodman tour as a "grabber" in marketing Ethel's other albums. However, as if to remind fans that she was still around when she returned home, Capitol released the second album under the title of *Have You Forgotten?*

Ethel's attitude toward the whole matter was one of passive acceptance. She just thought that's the way the business was, so why fight it? But the fact is that Ethel *was* in Brussels with Goodman and here again Westinghouse stepped in to save the day. On the film that they produced, Ethel *was* preserved for posterity, although at times she wishes she weren't. When she finally saw the film years later, she couldn't believe *that person* was her.

"There I was, standing up there in front of the microphone with no life, just singin' the words 'I've got a right to sing the blues, I've got a right to feel low down.' I was numb and unconscious—in a vacuum—kind of just there. I was inexperienced in expressing myself, so I was just using the voice, singin' the words, but not living them. It was Benny Goodman's repertoire, not mine, so the words didn't mean anything to me." Ethel goes on to say, "I sang it like I was in church." (Could this have been the old, familiar religion versus the blues conflict that Honey had drummed into Ethel's teenaged mind?)

There is a lot of mystery clouding what happened after Ethel's return. Admirers and supporters were waiting for a follow-up that would pack a wallop. They were waiting for that elusive "something" that would finally put its stamp of approval on their gal and let them know that their faith had been justified. But there was no jet-propelled skyrocket to instant stardom; what actually occurred more closely resembled one of those frustrating displays of Fourth of July fireworks that sends off loud blasts of explosives and a few promising sparkles here and there, but seems to lack some key element to powerfully thrust the darn thing off the ground. But in Fourth of July firework displays there are usually back-up supplies on hand; in the case of a performer's career, there are very few opportunities like the one Ethel had with Benny Goodman.

So there was reason for some questions. In a revealing interview with Ethel written six years after the tour, the mystery still continued. A columnist referring to Brussels commented: "By all conventional standards, Ethel had her big break . . . With this combination of right voice and right break, Ethel ought to be right up there with the greats . . . So what did happen, Ethel?" Ethel replied, "What happened? I couldn't say. Maybe it was mismanagement . . . I had just been married [shortly] before the Goodman tour . . . Maybe I just didn't want to go too far afield . . . But to tell the truth, I never was offered anything."

Further on in the article, Ethel refers to her relationship with the Red Fox and acknowledged that the club gave her "a false sense of security" and that as much as she cared for Fox the person, she felt that ". . . he was sincere, but limited." The article appeared in 1964 when Ethel was in another phase of her career and seemingly ready for a fresh, new start.

Today, in 1984, twenty years after that interview, Ethel views the Goodman tour through the perspective of the mature performer she has evolved into and offers an interesting insight: "Back then, I hadn't made up my mind about singing. I hadn't taken a stand on my career. My attitude was that I was just going along and enjoying it. There was *no commitment* or conviction behind it at all."

There is one last thing to consider. When Ethel had been chosen for the Benny Goodman tour, she was twenty-five and had been around the fringes of the business for eleven years, developing her own unique way of delivering a song. What did Benny hear in Ethel? Where was he coming from? A fair guess might be that he heard the promise in the voice and he also heard a performer who could enhance the kind of music he had made famous—swing. And swing had already seen its best days. She was a new talent in an old idiom, and as excellent as that idiom was, it was being replaced by totally new sounds and directions in pop music. In short, Ethel's kind of singing was out before she ever came in commercially.

With Goodman, Ethel had caught onto the tail end of a passing trend. To complicate matters further, she wasn't established enough yet to be one of those "legendary" singers who was keeping alive a musical tradition. So it was a case of talent with nowhere to go and no commitment to getting there. This perplexing question—where's the proper niche in the recording industry for this particular talent?—would cause some serious head scratching further down the line.

After Ethel's return to the States, she herself was not disappointed with the way things were going. She really expected nothing, so she just went passively along and took whatever life delivered to her. And for Ethel life always seemed to turn up something special. In the summer of '58, she attended a concert at Morgan State College in Baltimore. The headliner was another ambassador with a horn, the incomparable Louis Armstrong. The next thing she knew, Ethel *happened* to be on stage performing a duet with Louis. "There I was sittin' at the concert," Ethel recounts, "when someone noticed me and sent word that Ethel Ennis, who had just returned from a tour with Benny Goodman, was in the audience. I was requested to come up and sing."

Later during that same summer, Ethel rubbed shoulders with more greats of jazzdom when she did a gig at New York's Village Vanguard, a true haven for serious afficionados of the art. Ethel's trio consisted of Al Hall on bass, Kenny Dennis on drums, and Jimmy Jones (Sarah Vaughan's former keyboardist) on piano. Featured on the same bill was some more mind-boggling talent: the Miles Davis Sextet. On the bandstand with Miles were Cannonball Adderly on alto sax, John Coltrane on tenor sax, and a rhythm section of Bill Evans on piano, Jimmy Cobb on drums, and Paul Chambers on bass. As the *New York Mirror* (July 22, 1958) noted:

> Miles Davis' Sextet swings into the Village Vanguard tonight for two weeks with Benny Goodman's protege, Ethel Ennis, debutting locally with the warbling ability she presented at the Brussels World's Fair . . . .

One evening after work at the Vanguard, Jimmy Jones invited Ethel to another hotbed of jazz, Birdland, renamed nine years earlier in honor of tenor saxman Charlie "Bird" Parker. While they were there, Sarah Vaughan *happened* to be there as well. The two divas were introduced, but at that meeting they barely exchanged a brief "hello"; yet, at a later time they would exchange their respective albums.

A year later Ethel tackled the "workhouse" once again when she appeared on the Apollo bill with another musical Baltimorean, Cab Calloway. And then in August, 1959, a little more than a year after she had returned from her first European tour, she was off again overseas for a month-long engagement at the Astor Club, a classy room in London.

This time Ethel traveled solo. There was no big entourage, no lush champagne receptions, no crackerjack schedule to meet. There was time to look around and take it all in. And what she took in was a London ready to leap off into the sixties with wild abandon. Already the sounds from the north were filtering their way down into the London air. Hundreds of young groups in England and particularly in Liverpool had been involved for several years in something called the "skiffle" craze. Spearheaded by banjo player Lonnie Donegan, skiffle featured a variety of such homemade instruments as washboards, jugs, combs, and whatever else could be found that would make a sound. The movement attempted to recreate the strains of early black American blues and jazz as they were originally performed.

Although we didn't hear much about skiffle in this country, the term was American and originated in 1929 when singer Charley Spanel recorded a country blues called "Homemade Skiffle." Ironically, nearly all of the British super-rock groups had *their* roots in skiffle, which of course had *its* roots in black American blues and jazz. It seemed as if no matter where one turned in the realm of popular music, there at the foundation of it all stood the black American influence. But somehow the raw authenticity of this music and the people who created it were not, until very recently, widely acceptable to the world-at-large. And jazz, even now, never seems to capture the devotion of any but a relatively small handful of followers. This fact had a pervasive influence on Ethel's career.

In 1959, while Ethel was "taking in" London, a hard-hitting musical group of young men were gigging on weekends in town halls in Bootle, Garston, and Litherland, areas just outside of Liverpool. Their audiences were usually Teddy Boys who traveled in gangs armed with chains, knives, and steel-tipped boots and with their girls who were called "Judies." The Teds made great sport out of hassling the band and starting violent brawls. Their gestures were not merely empty threats. During one such encounter in the summer of '59, while the band was on the parking lot preparing to leave, the Teds started an ugly row. Most of the members of the group managed to get away, but small and frail Stu Sutcliffe, the bass player, was not as fortunate. Steel-tipped boots kicked him into bleeding unconsciousness. The other boys managed to get him home, and although he recovered, several years later he died—from causes directly attributable to that evening of insanity. The group's name back then was the Silver Beatles. Five years later they would literally set the world on its ear as they marshaled in the third great pop explosion.

Ethel felt the effect of the times; London was an eye-opener. "Traveling alone, I would be approached as prey for anyone, but then I became friends with an East Indian guy and he became my protector. As I walked around the streets, I saw the kids walking barefooted and I noticed that their attitude was a lot freer than back home. The guys had long hair, a fad which hadn't come to this country yet, and they dyed and bleached it in shocking colors."

Londoners, at least the audiences at The Astor Club, didn't fit in any way Ethel's picture of the prim and proper British. "Singin' all my nice songs, they didn't like those, but when I would sing my off-color songs, that's what brought the house down."

A bright spot and a source of comfort to Ethel on the trip was the friendship offered to her by the great singer Johnny Hartman. Hartman was living in London at the time and had played The Astor, too. On an off night, he invited Ethel to his house for a welcome, "home-cooked" meal.

By the time the sixties arrived, Ethel Ennis was in mid-career, having been in the business for thirteen years. The three years that followed were a bridge to the next step along the way. There was nothing terribly dramatic or dynamic that emerged from this period, just some minor rumblings here and there. Basically the next several years consisted of doing the night club circuit. The rooms continued to get better; there was a six-month gig at an East Side supper club in New York called The Toast and a few bookings in Philadelphia, but nothing that could be construed as a major breakthrough.

In her personal life there was a definite shift. Ethel began to stay away from home more frequently. She came back to Baltimore on her day off and took care of the house and marriage, but by this time Leeds had already received his state appointment and didn't appreciate it one bit when he would occasionally be referred to as "Mr. Ennis." Nonetheless, they added a new member to the household: "Lady Day" had come to stay, only in this incarnation she took the form of an English cocker spaniel. A few years later when Miles Davis came to visit, Lady Day didn't care if he *was* one of the great jazz trumpeters of all time; she bit him anyway. As Ethel tells it: "He said in this deep raspy voice of his, 'That crazy dog bit me!' And his finger *was* bleedin'. . . ." (Was Billie trying to communicate something to Miles from the great beyond?)

By 1963 Ethel had worked herself into a comfortable niche as a local celebrity and as such seemed to find a way to bring the greats to her. She did this with Louis and Miles, and in the summer of '60, she did it again with "The Count." Basie came to town for a concert at the Fifth Regiment Armory, and Ethel, along with blues singer Joe Williams, shared the bill with him.

On the recording front, there was very little action; it had been five years since Ethel had cut a record. Even so, *Playboy* magazine had acknowledged her as "one of the outstanding jazz artists" in their 1960 "All Star Jazz Poll."

By now a familiar routine had settled in that caused Ethel to exhibit some signs of restlessness—or perhaps talent has a mind of its own. She broke the relationship with George Fox for several months when she became associated with another "Fox" named Ray, a dapper young Philadelphia businessman who took over her management. It was short lived, but just long enough to wean her away from the security of her father figure—loyal and dedicated George. During this brief period Ethel severed her ties with the Red Fox, but within several months she was performing there again.

Life seemed to have come to a standstill reminiscent of those high school days just before Sylvester Coles showed up and invited her to join Riley's Octet. And in some ways, things hadn't changed very much at all. During this time Ethel was ambivalent about her talent, her marriage, and her life in general. The people and music that were out there making all the noise seemed very remote from Ethel Ennis, the jazz singer. Clearly she hadn't taken hold of the reins, nor had she expressed any commitment to building a career; it just kind of all flowed, unconsciously.

Once again, it could have ended for Ethel Ennis right there at the corner of Pennsylvania and Fulton Avenues except for one of those miraculous events that always *happened* to occur. As if on schedule, the next "great white father" appeared at the very moment he was needed to guide Ethel to the next step.

Darling Daughter in TV Debut

Ethel's first local television exposure was on WAAM' "It's High Time" talent show when she was seventeen (*above*). She won with her rendition of "The Man Love." An all expense paid trip to Philly to compete on "Paul Whiteman's Teen-Age TV Show," was part of the prize, courtesy of WAAM. Just prior to her departure with Bell, the *Baltimore Afro American* ran this photo in their issue of August 12, 1950 (*left*).

While still living in the projects on Gilmor Street, Ethel started playing and singing with Riley's Octet as the only female member of the all-male band. Shortly after that, she discovered her ability to write tunes. Shown here at eighteen with collaborator William Everhart from Dundalk, the pair had their song, "Little Boy" picked up by Savoy, one of the "sepia" labels based in New York. It was recorded by several singers including Little Richard.

By the early fifties, Ethel was leading a double life. She worked with The Tilters *(above)* by night and pursued a two year business course at Cortez W. Peters Business College by day. Ethel is pictured in the middle of the top row at her graduation in June, 1952 *(below)*. In tiny typeface the ad on the left proclaims The Tilters as "The Nation's Hottest Sepia Band." While she was with The Tilters Ethel began to get a taste of the low life in what she calls, "raw white places and raw black places."

One of the guys who acted as Ethel's protector during the rough and raw years was The Tilters' bassist, Arthur Nelson. Ethel developed a school girl crush on him, but it was short-lived when she discovered that she wasn't his one and only. His protection came in handy, nonetheless, when they played spots like the Flamingo *(above)* on Baltimore Street in the city's X-rated district.

After The Tilters disbanded, Ethel played and sang with the JoJo Jones Ensemble. That's JoJo on the guitar above, a man of extreme moods. His wild temper eventually created dissension in the group and they split up a year later. The bass player was Montell Poulson. He and Ethel later formed a musical duo. The crazy angle of the print was apparently Clinton's Studio's attempt to be "arty." In another arty attempt, the photographer had Ethel pose for some early "cheesecake." The photo (*left*) was taken right before her twenty-first birthday in 1953.

RED FOX LOUNGE

1st and Last Stop On The Avenue

Proudly Presents

SOMETHING NEW AND INTIMATE IN THE LINE OF
ENTERTAINMENT

7—NIGHTS WEEKLY—7

Featuring

ETHEL
ENNIS
ON THE
KEYS

MONTY
POULSON
ON BASS

They will win you over with their wonderful repertoire of new and
captivating songs
So Guys Bring Your Queens
and
Girls Bring Your Kings
and be enraptured by their refreshing personalities

Our kitchen is open until 1:30 A. M. for the finest food—from a sandwich
to a meal—under supervision of Bobby Cooper, formerly of the Tijuana
SPECIAL AT ALL HOURS—CHICKEN IN A BASKET
PACKAGE GOODS STORE—OPEN SUNDAY
SHOW TIME—9 UNTIL   SUN. MATINEE—7 UNTIL

RED FOX LOUNGE   *"First and Last Stop on the Avenue"*
COR. FULTON & PENNSYLVANIA AVES.

By 1954, Ethel had been discovered by George and Reba Fox, proprietors of
a jumping local establishment, the Red Fox. The club was one of the few
integrated spots in the city during that era. The Red Fox became Ethel's home
base for nearly a decade.

The sight of Ethel Ennis tickling the ivories and warbling her tunes on the small stage at the Red Fox brought joy to a growing following. Many a customer would while the night away nursing down one drink, much to George Fox's chagrin, while Ethel rendered her mellow jazz-flavored ballads.

Under Fox's management, Ethel began to take out-of-town bookings along the east coast. In 1956 she was playing places like Teddy Powell's Lounge in Newark, New Jersey. Ethel is shown here *(top)* with patrons of the club and dressed to the nines with members of the house group *(middle)*. Ethel takes a breather *(below)* with a book of crossword puzzles while playing a club in Cleveland during this same period.

orge Fox loved to host celebrations
nearly anything *(opposite, top)*.
re Ethel shares her cake with first
band, Attorney Jacques (Jack)
ds while smiling George looks on.
e portrait was a gift to Ethel from
l artist, Melvin Rudasill. Other
formers would sometimes join Ethel.
y Chambers hits the ivories, while
y Foxx and Ethel provide vocals
h back-up on bass by Poulson *(oppo-
bottom)*.

el's second recording was a single
the ATCO label. A newspaper ad
, *left)* and the publicity shot *(bot-
, right)* are reminders of early mar-
ing attempts. Above, Mr. and Mrs.
ds appear to be drinking a toast to
record's success.

Ethel boards a plane bound for the Brussels World's Fair in 1958 with the Benny Goodman A Stars (*above*). Vying with a bevy of hopefuls, Ethel was selected by Goodman for the covet female vocalist spot. She sang her way through sixteen European cities such as Cologne, Germa (*opposite, top right*) and palled around with her male counterpart, legendary blues singer, Jimm Rushing (*opposite, top left*). Royal treatment awaited the group everywhere as shown by the servi and spread offered Ethel in Hannover, Germany (*opposite, bottom*).

KURT LAUBER, MUNICH

PETER FISCHER, COLOGNE

BEI ABDRUCK, HANNOVER

Veilinggebouw klaar om taak van Carnegiehall over te nemen

Tuindersdorp BLOKKER wacht vol spannin op Benny Goodmans band

The Dutch newspaper, *De Volksrant* in Amsterdam *(above)* ran this feature article in their issue on May 10, 1958 as the little village of Blokker prepared to honor the group with the kind of welcome usually reserved for royalty. Featured in the article was a shot of Ethel rehearsing with Rushing. Goodman is seen in the lower left corner. In Oslo, Ethel enjoys a Scandinavian delicacy *(left)*. The group may have gotten tired, but they never went hungry.

Shortly after her return from Brussels, Ethel was requested by audience members to sing with Louis Armstrong, another ambassador with a horn, when he appeared at Morgan State College in Baltimore in July, 1958.

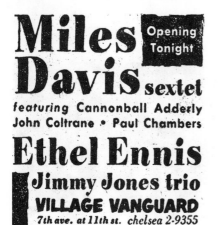
In August, 1958 Ethel appeared on tl
bill at the Village Vanguard, a hav
for jazz lovers. The ad in the *New Yo*
Mirror (left) announces Miles and Eth
loud and clear. In small print, la
giants of jazz, John Coltrane and Ca
nonball Adderly are mentioned. Eth
lulls the audience at the Village Va
guard *(bottom)* while keyboardi
Jimmy Jones takes over the piano. Jor
was formerly with Sarah Vaughan.

MARIO SANS, NEW YOF

The Apollo advertised itself as "Harlem's High Spot" and the "World's Greatest Colored Shows" during its first fruitful lifetime from 1943 until 1976. Virtually all of the greats of jazz had their rites of passage at the Apollo. Handbill *(above)* advertises "singing starlet" Ethel Ennis along with headliner Cab Calloway, another pride of Baltimore. Photos at right were shot Apollo-style and provide a collage of the many moods of Ethel Ennis as well other action on the stage. Earlier this year, 1984, the Apollo celebrated its tieth anniversary and reopened its doors for business as usual.

By the early sixties, Ethel had been in the business for thirteen years. Over and over, she was spoken of in the same breath with Ella Fitzgerald, Billie Holiday, Peggy Lee, and Sarah Vaughan. But fans were growing restless for the big break, which had yet to manifest itself. Here Ethel relaxes between sets in a New York supper club on the East Side called, the Toast.

V   *This is Ethel Ennis*

BY 1963 Ethel Ennis had attracted a cult-like following in Baltimore. Shery Baker, always faithful, even today, served as head of her fan club. "Ennis enthusiasts" (a term coined by Baltimore columnist John Goodspeed) would follow her on gigs up and down the East coast and continued to push for her recordings to be aired on local radio stations. As far as this "in" group was concerned, Baltimore was in the throes of spawning another legendary jazz singer, the greatest since Billie Holiday.

But Ethel herself backed away from calling her style "jazz"; she called it "progressive pop." "I hate to sing any song the way it's written—that's progressive. I'll use a jazz backing, but I think it's rather subtle." Even today Ethel is adverse to having her singing pigeonholed into any one particular musical style, most especially jazz. It's not that Ethel has anything against jazz *per se,* but she does feel that the term, which is greatly misunderstood anyway, is one that is constricting and doesn't adequately give space to the breadth of her versatility. Quite simply, Ethel wants to sing it all.

Regardless of how her singing was defined, Ethel's growing public loved to hear it. So it's not surprising that the next breakthrough in her career reads like the classic Hollywood scenario of a star is born. The script goes something like this. The New York manager comes to town. Someone says, "Hey, I want to take you to this little club to hear a *great singer.*" The manager agrees; he's always on the lookout for a great new discovery. He walks into the club and takes a listen. Wow! This lady is marvelous! She's really got it! He even imagines that he's possibly discovered the next Billie Holiday or Ella Fitzgerald. He keeps this in mind and checks her out again in a classier out-of-town room. This time he's even brought along an executive of a major recording label. They both concur: she's "hot stuff." He approaches her and offers her a contract. The young lady stares ahead dreamily and breathes a sigh of relief. At last—her big break has finally arrived! (The camera pulls back for a long shot and the jazzy music track soars to a breathtaking crescendo. . . .)

That's how it happens in Hollywood and that's how it happened to Ethel Ennis—well, almost. All of the facts are accurate with one exception: in the Ennis version, the starlet was *not* thrilled beyond belief to have her dreams of stardom answered at last. As Ethel tells it: "I was *not* there to be discovered. I never put myself in those places *just* to be *seen*; I was just singin' and enjoyin' myself. I didn't realize what this manager represented. I didn't attach anything to his offer at all since I never had the dream or the desire to become a star."

Ethel insists that when the contract was offered to her and even after she signed with Gerard (Gerry) Purcell, the manager in question, she was totally unaware of the magnitude of the opportunity. It wasn't until she was caught up in the heat of the business that what he was offering became more clear to her. At first she was unaware that she was now being placed in the same league with Purcell's other clients whose names at that time were household words in certain circles—Eddie Arnold, Al Hirt, Gretchen Wyler, Sally Ann Howes, and Gale Garnett. She was unaware that Purcell's firm, G. W. Purcell Associates, was in business only to build successful careers in the entertainment industry for its artist-clients, nor was she aware that he had a strong network of associates who handled the nuts and bolts of delivering "talent" to the marketplace. Gerry Purcell's connections included the prestigious William Morris Agency (bookings for club dates, TV appearances, jazz festivals, etc.); the highly regarded RCA Victor label (for recording contracts and related promotion and publicity); and a West Coast office in Hollywood. Although it seems incredible that Ethel didn't understand the value of the offer from the outset, even today she insists that she went ahead blindly.

Purcell, on his side, was unaware of the depth of his new client's naivete. Although he was relatively new in the business at the time, he was in the game as a full-fledged professional. This was an important shift of emphasis from Ethel's prior managers, who had jumped into the business solely on her behalf. In fact, Ethel had grown used to a bit of pampering and special attention. With the exception of those beginning years when she gigged in the "dives" around town, Ethel, as an artist, led a relatively sheltered and protected life. Her "great white father" and the guys in the band always seemed to want to protect her from the evil influences of the "devil's den." But the "big time" as she would come to discover, was big *business* as well, and many in the industry had no interest in either pampering or protecting artists, unless the artist began to show some promise of becoming a superstar—then all the rules were different. The bottom line, as offensive as it may be to an artist's ego, is called profit and loss, an important reality to keep in mind.

Those around Ethel viewed Purcell's offer as the chance of a lifetime, the big break into the magic kingdom of "show biz." What is it about this world that transmits such a compelling mystique? Its seductive power seems to reach out and weave its spell around even the ordinary mortals among us, those who secretly yearn to bask in the rewards of its glittery light. When Ethel Ennis approached its golden shores, the loyal and the faithful cheered her on. With her success, they too seemed to have vicariously fulfilled some apparently unattainable desire for fame and fortune. As for Ethel, her attitude about this new development was a low key: "I just went along to see what would happen. I thought it was all routine." Routine or not, when the contract arrived in the mail in June, 1963, Ethel Ennis signed on the dotted line as Purcell's client. Without knowing it, with that choice, she just *happened* to place herself on the road to stardom and fame and fortune.

Meanwhile, career conflicts were surfacing more than ever and led to marital unrest. Leeds was committed to his own career and to gaining a name for himself. *He* held a very high political position in the state for a black man, and yet *his wife,* the entertainer, was capturing all of the attention. Nonetheless, the Leeds decided to buy their own home—their first— on Leighton Avenue in northwest Baltimore. They moved into the house on August 28, 1963, the same day that Dr. Martin Luther King, Jr. delivered his stirring "I have a dream" speech, which envisioned equal rights for Black Americans. The ownership of the house, which later reverted solely to Ethel, was the fulfillment of one of her own dreams. ("Mama always told me to buy property. She said it was a good investment.")

So while Ethel Ennis had put *her money* on her *house,* Purcell, like George Fox before him, was ready to put *his money* on *Ethel Ennis.* With the signing of the contract, Ethel had unknowingly become a partner in the symbiotic relationship that exists between talent and management, whereby the livelihood of each depends on the other. At thirty, Ethel had definitely hit the big time and at that level the stakes and the demands became very high. "In the beginning," Ethel recalls, "it seemed to be the same thing I was always doing, only now it was on a national level."

Apparently nobody told Ethel the facts of show biz life. Nobody told her that talent is cheap in the business, only a small part of a much bigger package. Nobody told her that far more important were qualities like commitment, desire, self-awareness, and business sense. Nobody told her, as harsh as it may have sounded, that what she was entering into was a commercial enterprise—a business venture. Traditionally these two areas, business and art, have mixed together like oil and water. The questions were the same then as now—where does one draw the line between products manufactured for the marketplace and true artistic integrity? How far can one go in the one direction without risking failure in the other? These were the issues that Ethel would begin to meet face-to-face in the next few years. Until now she had been "playing around" with her gifted vocal chords. With this move her talent was on the line.

In some ways it was like starting all over again. Not since her Capitol days, before the Goodman tour in 1958, had Ethel cut a recording. This time the label was the powerful RCA Victor organization. These guys spared no expense to get behind their artists and build them into major stars—and they had the bucks and the brains to do it. They pulled out all stops by placing full-page ads in magazines, flooding the market with press releases, and setting up full-scale national promotion tours for their budding artists. And now Ethel Ennis, the "mild child" from Baltimore, was one of the rising stars on RCA's roster of talent.

By late 1963 Purcell gave Ethel the word: "The first thing we have to do is to concentrate on getting a recording out there. I've set up a meeting for you with Sid Bass, the arranger-conductor on the album. You'll meet him and go over the material." Although the liner notes imply that Ethel had dug deep and hard to find the gems on the album, in reality it didn't happen that way. The tunes were actually selected by RCA's A&R (artists and repertoire) department: in other words, the producer.

Ethel and Sid met and discussed the material, and he released the lead sheets to her while Ethel presented him with a number as well—"Nightclub," a tune she had collaborated on with fellow Baltimorean Bill Brooks. It became the only song with a blue note anywhere on the album.

With lead sheets in hand, Ethel returned to Baltimore to practice the songs while Bass worked out the scores and arrangements. A short time later Purcell contacted Ethel with the recording date and instructions to report to Webster Hall, ready to go. This was the studio that RCA and others used to acoustically accommodate their lavish productions; for scaled-down recordings, they used their own studios A and B.

On the specified date, Purcell was on hand at Webster Hall as were Sid Bass and a complete orchestra of strings, woodwinds, and rhythm section. Ethel's voice was in fine form, and as she prepared to record, she looked over in the control booth and uttered in surprise, "Hey, there's Wiswell."

And Wiswell it was, the same Andy Wiswell who had produced her albums at Capitol. A comfortable feeling of familiarity came over Ethel; she knew she had a friend at the controls. It was Wiswell, while they were at Capitol, who had shown her the ropes of the recording world. He taught her how to perfect microphone techniques, educated her about the sessions, and introduced her to songwriters. As Wiswell remembers it: "I was delighted to know that I would have such a great singer for my first RCA record. I had picked a repertoire which I thought would show off the marvelous variety of singing for which Ethel was capable."

Wiswell eventually went on to produce more than thirty Broadway cast albums; this was his forte. Of the twelve tunes on Ethel's first RCA album, more than half of them were from that genre; the remaining numbers were ballads old and new (at that time). The title of that initial album was *This Is Ethel Ennis,* but today Ethel says, "Back then it really *wasn't* Ethel Ennis. It was what *they* wanted me to sing. I felt like I had no choice, so they could call it *This Is Ethel Ennis* all they wanted to and it really wasn't me, who I really am. *I'm* the only one who can say, '*This* is Ethel Ennis' and mean it—and I didn't say it back in those days because I didn't know *who* or *what* I *really* was."

To add to this identity crisis, Ethel's authentic roots were jazz, and jazz was a loser in the marketplace. For example in 1979, while rock pulled in a hefty 41.2% of all record sales, jazz straggled greatly behind, accounting for only 3.8% of the market (National Association of Recording Merchandisers survey). It's no wonder that Ethel had a "thing" going on about being a jazz singer. Just as the church through Honey and Mama dictated her musical choices during her childhood, this time record sales were the determining factor.

Representing the industry's point of view, Purcell recently offered his insights: "It takes longer to develop a jazz singer. It's not commercial enough, so it's a problem for record companies. RCA was trying to develop a jazz-pop crossover, a middle-of-the-road product. Purist jazz is limited. Purists feel that they're selling out when they cross over, so it's a purist versus pop dilemma. Ethel felt more comfortable with jazz-oriented material at that time."

Since the beginning of Ethel's career, the question of marketing her style so that it would neatly fit into one category or another has been a source of confusion for record companies and Ethel herself. In the industry if a singer's style can be labeled and identified, it makes the marketing job much easier. On the other hand, classifying the work also places a limit on the artist, unless he or she has developed a personal style that transcends all boundaries. This aspect of artistic development, however, is the ultimate creative quest and may take a lifetime to develop.

Back in the mid-sixties, Ethel was not looking for a personal style of her own; she was simply interested in what she wanted or didn't want to sing. And RCA was interested, appropriately, in the marketplace. They thought they had a good thing in Ethel Ennis, provided they could discover the magic formula for an Ennis hit record.

The first album, while not a hit, was beautifully arranged and orchestrated. It had a lush, big production quality about it. Ethel's renderings were masterfully handled, especially on her own and Bill Brooks' composition, "Nightclub." Both the melody and lyrics paint a disturbing picture of the creatures who inhabit the empty, glazed-over realm of bars and nightclubs. The last verse sums up its message:

> While junkies drift in spheres unknown,
> They announce themselves with an occasional moan,
> While the till rings and a voice sings.
> We are all very much alone.

That last line of the song may have reflected more of the truth than Ethel ever realized. The country-at-large was in a state of radical change. Old institutions, traditions, and belief systems were breaking apart faster than our minds could handle it. President Kennedy was talking about putting a man on the moon by the end of the decade. For many, this Space Age dialogue was incomprehensible and even a waste of good money. But out of the Space Age research came the bits and pieces of advanced knowledge that have become the undergirdings of the high-tech society that we inhabit today. And the music industry, along with every other industry, was irreversibly affected by these developments.

During this same period, the Supreme Court on July 17, 1963, banned the recitation of *The Lord's Prayer* or *Bible* verses in the public schools. Ironically, in the same year, as if to keep it alive somewhere, the Mormon Tabernacle Choir hit gold (500,000 records sold) with their version of *The Lord's Prayer.*

Generally speaking, the prevailing mood of the country became one of, "Science is in; spirituality is out!" As far as many people were concerned, God was dead. And so we looked for comfort elsewhere, like the creatures in "Nightclub," as we searched for new gods to worship. As one Indian guru said, "The avatar (manifestation of God's spirit) has to come to the children of the Dark Age (America) in the form of a chemical. . . ." And it did, in a multitude of forms—LSD, PCP, marijuana, cocaine, etc.

However, no matter how high anybody was that November in '63, they came down with a stunning jolt with the news of Kennedy's assassination. If we thought, "We are all very much alone" before the tragedy, his death deepened our sense of loss even more and left us floundering, directionless. As the dark winter passed, we were ready for something to come along and brighten our spirits. And *the* something was to show up in the form of those four irreverent and brilliant young men from England, who now called themselves simply—The Beatles. However, they weren't due to touch down on American soil for several weeks yet.

Meanwhile, in early 1964 RCA set up an extensive promo tour to introduce its latest find to key market areas throughout the United States. One of the first stops was Boston. Here *Boston Sunday Globe* columnist Harvey Siders (January 26, 1964) captured the essence of Ethel's musical life at that time:

> You glance around the banquet room of the Boston hotel to which you've been invited. There's a small bar in one corner, and there's also a long buffet table boasting all sorts of goodies from shrimp to knishes. There you spot disk jockeys, record distributors and members of the press. On the small bandstand up front a piano tuner is working on the instrument as a bass player, drummer and guitarist begin to set up. . . .

Clearly this was an event where the shapers of public opinion were gathered. These people had *heard them all,* and while they were willing to cheer on new talent, they were quick to spot empty platitudes as well. It was into this arena that Ethel entered, a vastly different world from her small-time Baltimore days. As Harvey Siders continued:

> . . . Miss Ennis makes her appearance stunningly attired in a street-length brocaded, kelly-green gown . . . She begins with "He Loves Me" and "As You Desire Me" both from her new album . . . Immediately you notice that she prefers the jazz-induced freedom of a small combo to the lush orchestral backing given her on the recording. . . .

He next elaborated on Ethel's performance style; her flair for humor; her impersonations of Billie Holiday, Sarah Vaughan, and Dinah Washington; her ability to change moods from a slow seductive ballad to a "gently pulsating swing number"; her clear grasp of the lyrics. He checked out the others in the room "to glean their collective reaction" and was "gratified when they burst into applause." Ethel had undoubtedly won the support of Boston. Siders inquired about her future plans. Ethel revealed that her schedule had been tightly organized with promos of the same sort in other cities, a series of meetings with disc jockeys, and in her spare time, appearances on TV. She also added, "It's exhausting, but that's the business and I love it as long as I can keep singing." And, "Oh, one more thing . . . I just want my head to be in the spotlight."

What was this? Our meek and mild Ethel wanting her head in the spotlight? Today Ethel says, "What I probably meant was that I wanted my *head* in the spotlight and not my *hips.*" (Ethel's hip area is her nemesis and well-meaning friends have given her the CB handle "Heavy Hips," but Ethel takes it all in good humor.) Whatever she meant by that comment, Ethel's head *was* in the spotlight in places such as New York's Village Gate in February, 1964.

During the very same moment that Ethel was playing "the Gate," a few miles away at Kennedy Airport, the third pop explosion had arrived. This one was called the British Invasion, and the nation was ready, willing, and able to get into the spirit of the Beatles' arrival. Interestingly enough, the Beatles got a lot of their inspiration, like Elvis before them and Sinatra before him, from the very same roots as Ethel: good old American jazz. But for the Beatles the white/black culture conflict was not the issue it was in this country, so they were creatively free to take the music wherever they wanted—and they did. In turn, we responded on a level approaching full-scale mania.

Meantime, reviews for Ethel were enthusiastic, although they were nearly overlooked in the Beatle blitz. Of her performances at the Gate, *Billboard* noted: "She has much poise, humor, swing, and much natural talent." Others agreed: "Ethel is made of the same kind of stuff that put Billie Holiday and Dinah Washington in a class by themselves. . . ." And: "Now that she has achieved some much deserved recognition, things will be looking up for both her and her listening public. . . ."

However, the next month in Los Angeles at the Crescendo ("During its *descending* days," Ethel wittily interjects), things were looking *down*. The house group was not up to Ethel's standards. She called the New York office requesting a change in musicians. Permission denied! So she hired suitable musicians, used her own salary to pay them, and cleared a net total of twelve dollars for the two-week engagement.

Of her performance at the Crescendo, *Variety* felt that she was an excellent technician and a perfect "disk thrush," but needed to learn "strong nitery showmanship." Ethel had spent most of her years as a single behind the piano, so she wasn't accustomed to being out in front. This became an issue with Ethel, something she needed to learn to adjust to as she went along. The reviewer also validated Ethel's own definition of her style as "progressive pop"—"primarily a ballad delivery . . . mixes it with a nice jazz flair."

Whatever the reviewers had to say about Ethel, be it praise or criticism, it never bothered her at all; she never was curious enough to read her reviews. The New York office provided her with a clipping service that sent to her any mention of her name in print on a regular basis, but she just wasn't interested. Nor did she bother to listen to and evaluate her own recordings. Honey had implied that it was vain to listen to her own voice. Recently Ethel has seen the folly of this advice and has come to realize that getting feedback from her own performances is a critical tool for her own growth and understanding.

In connection with her record promo, Ethel began appearing on national network television in March, 1964. The first stop was the "Steve Allen Show." As chance would have it, that was the same night that Tony Perkins was also a guest on the show. Perkins and Allen got involved in a foam lather battle and got so "into it" that the skit spilled over into Ethel's time and—splat—right onto her album cover. It seems that when Allen introduced Ethel's number, Perkins was seized with an irresistible urge to eject a stream of lather right onto her photo on the album's cover. The audience thought it was hysterical, but Ethel, already in place for her number, didn't know *what* was happening. Allen, a lover of musicians, came to his senses and offered an on-the-air apology.

While not as eventful as Allen's program, Ethel's other appearances within the next several months covered the route of late night and talk shows, plugging the songs on her album. Usually these appearances were sandwiched in between her gigs. She would do a taping anywhere between five to seven in the evening and then go off to do her show. On these programs, Ethel never did a sit-down guest appearance; she strictly performed her numbers. She recalls, "I never had anything to talk about in those days. I wouldn't have known what to say." In fact, Ethel had created such a convincing image of herself as a bland nonspeaker that Purcell also agreed that she should only sing on these programs. Today Ethel traces this syndrome back to that early childhood maxim that ruled the Ennis household: "Children should be seen, but not heard."

Meanwhile, *This Is Ethel Ennis* was coming along moderately well; it was time to cut album number two. Based on the results of the first album, RCA decided to try another approach. This time they eliminated the strings and went full steam ahead on the brass. There were some good numbers on the album: "Love For Sale," "I'm A One Man Woman," "Show Me A Man," and others. They called this attempt *Once Again, Ethel Ennis.* Obviously they wanted to get her name out there. Ethel, who has her own inimitable brand of wit, comments, "I thought to myself, 'Well, here I am *again.* Where were *you* the *first* time?'" Her choice of a title would have been *Ennis, Anyone?* But in those days, nobody asked "the star" for her opinion.

Nonetheless, Ethel had her say anyway, through the music itself. It all broke loose one hot summer day at the Eleventh Newport Jazz Festival. Even though rain clouds threatened all day long, eleven thousand fans thronged to Peabody Park in Rhode Island to see and hear the great jazz luminaries. Along with these stellar talents, some of the promising lesser known artists performed at the matinee sessions. Ethel Ennis was among the latter. For Ethel this was a routine gig. She was asked to report there by the office, so she didn't assign any special significance to Newport nor did she do anything out of the ordinary to get herself in shape.

But Newport *wasn't* just an ordinary gig. For one thing, the press was on hand from the major newspapers to cover the scene. For another, this was a *jazz* festival and was closer to the stuff on which Ethel had been nurtured and raised. She had a fine group of musicians to back her up: Cozy Cole on drums, Slam Stewart on bass, Billy Taylor on piano, and Walt Namuth on guitar. When it came Ethel's time to perform, the group let it rip with numbers like "The Song is You," "I Love Being Here With You," "But Beautiful," "Yesterdays," "Angel Eyes," and "I Only Have Eyes For You." She and the group created music that afternoon that had the aliveness, spontaneity, and freedom that she dearly missed in the recording studio.

When it was all over, the crowd and critics were amazed. They wanted to know, "Where did she come from? Why haven't I heard about her before? Where has she been hiding out?" In one fell swoop, with some ebullient praise from the critics, Ethel Ennis was hailed as a new discovery, a great fresh gift to jazz. *Down Beat,* the voice of jazzdom, dubbed her "the surprise of the 1964 Newport Jazz Festival." The *New York Times* followed suit: "A real high-spot of the afternoon was Ethel Ennis." And the *New York Herald Tribune* declared: "Her name is Ethel Ennis and she is a singer who is likely to develop into the No. 1 performer in her class . . . It was a thrilling performance, and . . . all jazz fans should keep at least one ear cocked in the direction of Ethel Ennis."

The fans didn't have to wait too long. RCA, unlike Capitol during the Brussels tour, grabbed onto the excitement of the moment. They were eager to capitalize on this sudden turn of events, and Ethel, for once, got her way with the artists and repertoire department on her next recording, *Eyes For You.* In reviewing the production of that album, Ethel says, "Now we were gettin' into slippers—you know, old house shoes. It was freer, different from the other albums and I felt at home." To cap the homey feeling, Ethel brought along some of her hometown musicians to record with her: Walt Namuth on guitar and Jimmy Wells on vibes. Gone from this recording were the big band, schmaltzy arrangements. *Eyes For You* attempted to recapture the spirit of Newport, and like the earlier *Lullabys for Losers,* it emphasized simple instrumental backup and the purity of Ethel's sound. The critics responded in kind. The album got lots of air play, was awarded four stars in *Down Beat,* and put Ethel's name in that publication's TDWR (Talent Deserving of Wider Recognition) section.

At the end of July, as if to cement that peak moment at Newport, Ethel was booked on the "Bell Telephone Hour" and performed with The

Duke himself. By this time, she had appeared with Goodman, Armstrong, Count Basie, Cab Calloway—and now, Ellington.

During her club dates, she continued to impress the critics at every stop along the way. At Mr. Kelly's in Chicago, the *Chicago Sun Times* (August 15, 1964) described Ethel as ". . . a smoldering jazz contralto with phrasing that leaps, lifts, or melts into a lovely dying fall. . . ."

While Ethel's *phrasing* may have had the adroitness of a dancer, her stand-up performance back then was still a little shaky. It was awkward for Ethel, who was used to using her piano as a "crutch," to stand totally exposed to the audience with nothing between them except a mike. The business had a solution to such a problem; it was called choreography lessons. This wasn't hard-core dancing instruction; it was closer to a coaching session in the art of movement on stage. From Purcell's point of view, this was perfectly justified: "Singers need to be able to do *more* than sing. In clubs, the sound is not usually as good as on the album, so a performance needs to be visually exciting, and the artist needs to be able to communicate with the audience. They don't lose anything by being an entertaining singer. They need to be more than a piece of cardboard up there. They can't be up there like a klutz; they have to move with ease and grace. That's what the choreography lessons are for."

Things had changed from those early childhood days when all Ethel wanted to do was dance and hated the "awful" piano lessons. "Purcell thought I needed choreographing badly. He wanted to take me away from the piano which had become my security, my safety valve. He was asking me to *reveal* myself—to remove this barrier. I wouldn't have a big piano to hide behind anymore, so I had to find out what to do with my hands, how to be personable on stage.

"So he sent me to a choreographer who could teach me how to move. He would play my records and tell me what gestures to use on certain words. It was awkward for me to have someone else telling me how to move. So even though the lessons were costing us thousands of dollars, which we split, I wasn't opened to it at all. So I told Purcell that I didn't like it and that I didn't want to do it."

And *that* wasn't all! According to Purcell, "An artist has to *look good.* Some singers may start out working in a smokey jazz room and they can be casual there, but when they go into the better clubs, they have to be groomed—not that they have to be show girls—but people are looking at them and they don't want to be repelled."

About this matter, Ethel recounts, "I was told never to sit down, as this would cause creases. It was important to be spiffy in front of people. I was even considering buying a slant board so my gowns wouldn't get mussed."

Ethel was beginning to feel the pressure of the big time. It was not a new feeling. Just as she had inwardly resented the piano lessons she was forced to take under parental domination, she now had a new "Mama" to answer to in the form of Gerry Purcell. He became a symbol for Ethel, an authority figure who represented the formula for developing artists into show biz packages. This was an area she was finding difficult to tolerate. "They were asking me to do things I didn't want to do. They told me to go to certain cocktail parties in order to be seen by 'the right people,' dress a certain way, set up an apartment in New York. They even suggested that I should have my teeth worked on. I didn't want to do those things—*they weren't me!*"

Sooner or later, all performers must confront these issues. For some the rewards are great enough to play the game; for others, the cost is far too high. Purcell views it this way: "The entertainment business is a world that demands *all-out commitment*—total dedication and sacrifice. There has to be a strong desire to the exclusion of everything else. It just can't happen without that sacrifice. Ethel was very hard to convince. She wasn't the easiest person to talk into changes."

Ethel's attitude was clear. "I told them that I wasn't interested in doing what they were asking me to do. I didn't feel that *their* way was right for me."

Purcell listened to her complaints, considered them, and then responded, "Well, I guess you don't want to be a star because these are the things you must do to be a star. I guess you want to be a semi-star."

The smoldering jazz contralto replied, "Well, then I guess I don't want to be a star—I'll be a semi-star."

Purcell recalled recently, "At the time, Ethel had a negative attitude about life—and herself!"

A large part of this negative attitude could be attributed to her marriage, which was rapidly heading toward divorce. Even though Ethel had tried her best to make it work, .the career conflicts that had been there all along were taking their toll on both marriage and career. It was a rocky time for Ethel. Unfortunately, during most of the first year and a half that she was with Purcell, she was going through the most painful upheavals of the impending divorce. The situation had its effect and intermittently took her needed attention away from the business.

Around this time Ethel also violated the contract on a three-night club date in New Jersey. It was a situation similar to the earlier Crescendo appearance where the house group was not up to her standard. But this time, at the end of the first evening, she simply walked off the job. Purcell was not pleased nor was the union, which threatened to, but never did, impose a fine.

For Ethel, show biz was beginning to look uncannily like that "devil's den" that Honey always talked about. Life for Ethel Ennis the talented, rising star and Ethel Ennis the shy, yet increasingly tenacious human being was becoming very confused. A lot of the issues that had been quietly building within her all along, since the beginning of her career back in the late 40s, were rapidly coming to the fore. Everything—her music, race, family and business relationships, and, most of all, her Self—was up for questioning. As Ethel said in a news quote from this period of her life: "It's hard I tell you: it's like being between the devil and the deep blue sea."

VI

Between the Devil
and the Deep Blue Sea

*T*HE WORLD of pop music in the mid-sixties had revved itself into a new level of high energy with an intensity unknown before in the industry. The British Invasion via The Beatles was in full swing, as was Berry Gordy, Jr.'s magic Motown sound. Rock 'n roll was *finally* being taken seriously by the major labels. And, while Woodstock was still a few years away (1969), rock groups had already started experimenting with sound, light, and drugs, as well as with gurus and exotic instruments. Music had become a potent force for political and social protest with artists like Bob Dylan, Paul Simon, the Rolling Stones, and others, who were a far cry from the fluffy sugar-coated tracks of mainstream tin pan alley. Assuredly the mainstream had a powerhouse to offer in Grammy Award winner Barbra Streisand, who copped the award for Best Contemporary Pop Vocal Performance by a Female from 1963 to 1965, the same years that Ethel was recording for RCA. And Aretha Franklin was waiting in the wings to capture the same award with her gutsy style for Best R&B Vocal Performance by a Female in 1967.

One thing was certain, the industry was alive and buzzing. Music was a big megabucks business, where wanting to "make it" counted as much, if not more, than having talent. As a recording artist, Ethel Ennis got lost

57

somewhere in the shuffle. Here was a gifted black singer who projected a sophisticated white sound on expensively produced albums of jazz-pop "safe" songs. While the voice was like a finely tuned musical instrument— crystal clear, wide-ranging, and sensitively pitched—*something seemed to be missing.* That "something" would take years for Ethel to discover.

In the meantime, she went on with what had become business is usual. In 1965, while appearing as a guest on Dave Garroway's "Nightlife" program, fellow guest Arthur Godfrey was so taken with Ethel that while they were still on the air, he invited her to appear as a guest on his show. She accepted, and for the next eight years she regularly spent two to three days a week in New York taping the show. Although Godfrey was a controversial figure, with as many enemies as friends, the exposure, for Ethel, was one of the most rewarding aspects of her career. She received fan mail from across the country and met an unending stream of well-known and talented guests who appeared on the program: Glenn Ford, James Whitmore, Daryl Zanuck, Phyllis Diller, John Davidson . . . the list goes on and on. Most of all, the connection with Godfrey's program allowed Ethel to keep her foot in the door of the New York scene, long after she had withdrawn from it in other ways.

Throughout the course of Ethel's career, there were inner forces at work as well as the circumstantial happenings of the music world. There was a three-way pull from her mother, her grandmother, and her ex-husband that kept Ethel from truly opening up and letting loose with everything she had. Grandmother Honey's strong religious views had a profound effect on Ethel, acting as a double-edged sword that lifted her up and kept her down simultaneously. "She always told me to be true to myself and to listen to my inner voice and it would tell me the right thing to do. She would say, 'When you feel it's wrong to do something, don't do it!' At the same time she placed restrictions on me."

After Ethel began to make recordings and TV appearances, Honey relented. "She saw that even though I was in 'the devil's den,' I still managed to remember my upbringing and remain a lady. And of course, when I started bringing home the money and helping financially, she began to look at it differently. She even gave me her *blessing.* And when she would look at me on TV, she was so proud, she was bustin' her buttons.

"Mama was another story. I felt she was proud, but I didn't get the full thrust of her proudness. There was sadness mixed in with it . . . and there was envy, too. Mama liked to be the center of attention, and I felt that by doing what I was doing I was taking the attention away from her, so I would go back into the background, become a shadow of myself. By me getting those 'vibes' from Mama—*maybe that's why I didn't want to go out there and be a big 'star.'* I felt it was almost like killing her.

"She always compared me with everybody on TV. I wasn't moving fast enough for her, not giving her enough money. She wanted to impose on me what *she* would do, instead of letting me do my own program."

Then there was Jack, her ex-husband, whom Ethel speaks of warmly today, but during their marriage, it was another matter: "The more recognition I got, the angrier he became."

In those days, Ethel had not developed her ability to openly confront and communicate her feelings about these matters, so she kept them hidden. However, feelings always seem to find a way to express themselves either through what we say or what we do. And what Ethel decided to do, especially about her growing discomfort in her relationship with Purcell, was to become involved with another manager.

John Powell, an easy-going gentleman from Spokane, Washington, who was in the booking and promotion end of the business, *happened* to show up while Ethel was appearing in Los Angeles at the Slate Brothers Club. In a pattern consistent with the three previous managers in her life, he was overwhelmed by her talent and thought he could be the one to give her the boost she needed to push her over the edge to stardom. Ethel did not take bookings with him immediately; Purcell, after all, did have a vested interest in her career. And the other artists in Purcell's stable were doing very well indeed with NARM (National Association of Recording Manufacturers) and Grammy awards to their credit.

But not Ethel Ennis. RCA executives were in a quandary about what it would take to make that break in the marketplace. Thus far they had tried big band with strings, big band without strings, and a simple combo arrangement. None of that made any difference it seemed. On their fourth time out with Ethel, they tried yet another approach. This time they used a variation of the combo. It was like an extended combo, with nine to eleven pieces including a harpsichord, a melodica, and some electronic instrumentation. Wiswell selected twelve well-known waltzes and had Dick Hyman arrange them in 4/4 time. The album was called *My Kind of Waltztime*. But the sales for this one were like the others: steady and slow-moving—as Ethel herself could be characterized back then (Perhaps there was a correlation between the artist's energy and album sales.)

In fact there *were* several singles that sold well, and one, "The Boy From Ipanema," even made the charts. But the recording industry is a mysterious business. No one has the answer to what will sell, although one thing *is* certain: *if* Ethel's records had made some noise in the marketplace, her entire career in show business would have been different.

RCA hung in there until the bitter end. There was one more recording session, and Purcell, although he rarely stepped into the recording end of the business in those days, had a request of Ethel. He handed her a song that he personally thought would be a winner. In looking back, Ethel recalls, somewhat wistfully, "He gave me this song from his hand to my hand in the studio at RCA. It was a beautiful tune called "Until It's Time For You To Go." I sang it and I looked over at him. I felt that he was disappointed in me. I felt that I could have given the song a better reading, but I hadn't experienced those feelings in my life yet, and I couldn't fake it."

Even today Ethel has a strong position about what she will and won't sing. As she says, "If I haven't experienced something in my life yet, I can't sing about it with conviction. And if it's something I don't stand for, why should I sing about it at all?"

The recordings that Ethel made at that last session were never released. She hasn't cut another recording on a major label since then. Whatever the reason, the truth is that Ethel never produced any recordings containing the "magic moment" that makes for a hit record. It just wasn't there.

By May, 1965, Ethel's divorce was final. It was also the same month that the *National Observer* (May 31, 1965) concluded that Ethel Ennis was a *singer's singer,* as Billie Holiday had predicted. What is meant by this term, which by the way carries a negative conotation? According to the article, a singer's singer is one who will be respected by singers, other musicians, and a few *cognoscenti,* but with odds "heavily against the possibility that many millions of people will like you." This poignantly written article describes Ethel's story as "a case study in what happens when a singer's singer and her backers decide she must become a public favorite."

The question that was to become Ethel's "hook" for the next nineteen years was put forth once again: "Then why is attractive 32-year-old Ethel Ennis not bumping the top along with, say, Nancy Wilson, who is no better a singer?" Intimates in the business responded with: "No public relations sense" and, after all, "She's just an ordinary girl who happens to be a singer," followed by "She's uncomfortable standing in front of the mike," to "She needs a little more friendliness with the public" and "She's no big pusher," and finally with comments on Ethel's own desire to be "all art" rather than "commercial." All of these explanations were very good theories at the time, and they may even have reflected a bit of the truth, but they were shortlived.

Less than a month after the *National Observer* article appeared, *Down Beat* took the opposite stand in applauding her performance at the Scene in Hollywood. In distinct contradiction to the singer's singer view of Ethel, the reviewer praised her for her ability to alternate between "the commercially desirable image that makes promotion-wise RCA Victor happy and the impish, yet sophisticated humor of the jazz-oriented singer that livens and lifts an intimate lounge." For Ethel the stint at the Scene was memorable for quite another reason. It was here that she met one of her long-time vocal heroines. "Peggy Lee stopped in to hear me sing. She was there to listen and she liked my version of 'The Boy From Ipanema'." This was high praise coming from a singer whom Ethel feels stylistically exudes the ultimate in sensuality. More than that, Ethel was impressed with the person. "I found her to be very warm. We talked and held hands. I felt a sisterhood between us as female singers."

That was in June, 1965. A few months later in August, there was no feeling of sisterhood or brotherhood between blacks and whites as thirty-five people lost their lives and millions of dollars of damage occurred during riots in the Watts area of Los Angeles. One year earlier, on June 29, 1964, the Civil Rights Act was passed. Discrimination in voting, housing, jobs, etc., was declared illegal and unconstitutional. But laws are only laws; they obviously don't have the power to change people's hearts. The jazz contralto, it seems, wasn't the only black who was smoldering; the entire mood of black America was escalating into one of anger and rage. The riots in Watts were only a beginning.

By fall, Ethel was back in New York at a club called the Living Room. Here again one of the earlier "theories" about her lack of acceptance was giving way. *Billboard* (September 4, 1965) stated: "Miss Ennis, already established as a top recording star, is also developing into a *fine club act*." (Apparently the choreography lessons, resistance or not, had taken hold.) The review continued: "The give and take between Miss Ennis and her audience *established a warm rapport*."

And then it was back to the West Coast again for another jazz festival, this time in Monterey. Joe Williams, who keeps cropping up in Ethel's life, was also there and he and Ethel performed a duet. But unlike Newport fourteen months earlier, this time Ethel's talent was no surprise to anyone. In fact the enthusiastic critical praise at Newport was replaced by a growing sense of frustration and impatience on the part of eagle-eyed Ennis watchers. As *Down Beat* (November 4, 1965) observed: "Miss Ennis continues to show great promise and one hopes that the promise will be fulfilled before too long."

This statement raises some thought-provoking questions about life. What is meant by "great promise"? Was Ethel in fact fulfilling it? What does it take to fulfill one's promise? Is this something we all possess in some way, or is it relegated to only a special few among us? These questions would take Ethel the better part of the next twenty years to answer for herself.

While she was still on the West Coast Ethel took some bookings that did little to hasten the big breakthrough. She did a production number, "I've Got That Feeling," for Scopitone, a forerunner of video music. This was a European import that could be compared to a video jukebox. When a quarter was inserted, the selection would pop up on the screen in full living color and sound. It was a clever idea, but like the Edsel, it didn't last. She also cut a title track for an animated motion picture that wasn't exactly a runaway smash at the box office. It was called *Mad Monster Party* and featured the voices of Phyllis Diller and Boris Karloff, among others.

If anything, by October, 1965, the monsters and the devils, the confusion and the pressure seemed to be having the party in Ethel's life. Ethel's conflicts with the show business environment continued to manifest themselves. Ethel says, "Every time Purcell started talkin' about me being a *star*, I felt that he was going to create something and I was afraid of that creation, that I wouldn't like who I would become. I felt like a puppet, like my freedom was gonna be snuffed out. It got real serious and it felt dark and heavy.

"I thought that they were gonna put more dressing on the outside and chip away at my inside. I wanted to be *whole*. I had seen other performers when they were no longer in the limelight, they seemed like lost souls— only because they didn't take time out to 'do time,' to develop the inner self. I didn't want that to happen to me.

"I felt that I had talent with nothing behind it, not enough experience of life to support it. I was afraid if I got that far and they lost interest, I would have no power of my own at all."

Purcell says, "There are stages of an artist's development. A lot of artists are afraid. They are afraid to make mistakes, but you've got to make mistakes if you want to develop."

Perhaps it was more a question of being afraid to take the risk or being afraid of the unknown or even being afraid of the temptations that await innocent little girls in the bad "devil's den." Even today, there is no way to convince Ethel that these were her own "devilish" projections. For her, even though she never "lost her soul," she is absolutely dead certain that given where her development was at that time, she surely would have. And who is to say whether or not her feelings were well-founded? All that matters is that for Ethel they were real at the time.

Given Ethel's own declaration that she was content with being a "semi-star," and the fact that the press had concluded that she would be artistically well-received as a "singer's singer" but would probably never reach wide public or commercial acceptance, it's no surprise that her career was becoming a bit precarious. Even so, being a semi-star and singer's singer is more than most of us achieve in our lifetimes. Perhaps these epithets were symptomatic of something deeper: Ethel's own fear and resistance to being a star or an entertainer. Even now she feels that the public has attached a lot of empty value to the glamour of it all and that these roles don't authentically reflect what her life has become. As she says, "People expect you to be a certain way if you're in show biz and that isn't who I am."

There is one more interesting piece to the puzzle of "How come Ethel Ennis never made it big in the big time?" Ethel, although she has trouble seeing herself as a jazz singer, has lived her entire musical and personal life as an expression of jazz. Her heart is jazz; her soul is jazz; and the way she thinks, feels, and operates in the world is jazz. Ethel likes to free-form her way through life. She loves spontaneity and playing with ideas as they come to mind. She also loves to play with words and improvise, even in normal everyday conversations. And until recently, she has always resisted tight form, structure, conventional discipline, or even writing anything down on paper. Ethel Ennis *is* jazz, even when the song she is singing is classical, spiritual, or the National Anthem. It is that way now and it was that way then. In short, Ethel didn't like the feeling of restraint that Purcell seemed to be putting around her life. So Ethel found someone in "the biz" whom she felt was more in line with her way of doing things: enter John Powell.

Shortly after Purcell started pushing for Ethel to seriously groom herself for stardom, Ethel started taking gigs with Powell. Powell was less demanding. In fact they never put anything down on paper regarding their business arrangement; it was more casual and relaxed than that. Powell offered Ethel bookings, mostly on the West Coast and in Canada. If she wanted them, it was OK; if not, it was OK, too. Powell split the commissions with Purcell's office, and even though Purcell says that he "never stood on ceremony," given what had already gone down, it may not have been a wise move.

Ethel's first booking with Powell was a concert at Pullman College outside of Spokane. It was to be a double bill with Jackie Vernon, but at the last moment Vernon canceled. In the meantime, just prior to departure while she was in the airport, Ethel became seriously ill. She was delayed getting to the concert and because of Vernon's cancellation, she felt compelled to go on. "I had a temperature of 103 degrees and a virus infection. I was so weak, I could barely stand up. The way it looked to some people in the audience, since I arrived late anyway, was that I was on some kind of drunk. Anyhow, I got through it and even got a standing ovation."

Whatever that attack was signaling to Ethel, she didn't pay it any attention. Several months later, again under Powell's management, Ethel was appearing in Vancouver at the Marco Polo Theater Restaurant. This time *while* she was performing she choked on her own saliva and couldn't breathe. "When I got back to the hotel I was hangin' out the window tryin' to get air in my lungs. Early the next morning I tracked down a medical center and I found out that I was having a serious asthma attack. I never had asthma before. But they gave me one of those inhalators and it fixed me right up."

Ethel has been singing her way through the asthma ever since.

Toward the end of 1965, Ethel was spending her time taping the Godfrey show, and flying from coast to coast for night club appearances. In November Powell booked her into a place that was to become one of her favorites, the Red Onion in Aspen, Colorado. Cradled in the sweeping Rocky Mountains, the "Onion" was a place where Ethel's appearances were greeted with phrases like "Ethel Ennis returns to the Red Onion for the -illionth time." Clearly the club had adopted her, as the Red Fox in Baltimore had done earlier in her career. However, this environment was a far cry from the now declining Red Fox. It was open and airy with an elegant rustic feel to it, and it was the "in" place to go in Aspen.

Year's end found Ethel on one of Purcell's bookings in the mecca of the entertainment world, Las Vegas. Rising out of the dust of the desert was the glitter, glamour and gambling paradise of America. At the luxurious Fremont Hotel, Ethel appeared as one of four headliners in the main room. The other acts were British singer Matt Monro, a comedian, and a dance act that opened the show each night as they kicked their way through "Seventy-Six Trombones."

For Ethel, Las Vegas was about visiting a fortune teller, Miss Rose. The occult is something that has always fascinated her, and to this day, Ethel has her own personal astrologer, tarot card reader, and occasionally visits a gypsy or two. Miss Rose had a few predictions to make and Ethel hung onto every word. "She told me that I would be taking a trip over water and that it would be a safe journey. She also saw a white man in my life who would be traveling with me sometime. The idea of any kind of relationship at that time was very remote. I hadn't healed from my marriage yet. And the red ace of diamonds kept comin' up. She said it meant money."

At least one of Miss Rose's predictions manifested itself rather quickly. As 1966 rolled in, Ethel was on a journey "over water," bound once again for London. This time she played a two-week engagement in a trendy Soho jazz cave called Annie's Room, another one of Purcell's bookings. About this off-beat side of London, Ethel recalls, "People who wanted more out of life came to Soho." One of those people was the great jazz pianist Errol Garner. Garner liked Ennis's style and the two befriended each other. Once when they were out together dining, a peculiar smell floated through the air. As Ethel tells it, "Errol started sniffing around and then I started to smell something too. That's when I discovered that we had something in common. One of us said, 'It smells like an asafetida bag. I used to wear one when I was a kid.' Well, we looked at each other and burst out laughing. 'You too?' We both said it at once. That made me feel closer to him; we had that childhood secret that we shared."

Soon after she returned home, Ethel started taking more bookings with Powell, and by spring she was splitting her bookings about fifty-fifty between the two managers. In April, during a Powell booking in Vancouver, *The Province* (April 27, 1966) stated: "Here is Ethel Ennis, milk chocolate laced with rum, carefully and meticulously placing her words with the softness, precision, and femininity of a ballet dancer." Once again, Ethel's vocal ability had been compared to that of a dancer, She seemed to have found a way to satisfy her urge to be a ballet dancer through the art form that she did develop, the medium of her own voice.

During this same engagement, Ethel finally met another one of her long-time musical heroines. If Peggy Lee is the ultimate in sensuality for Ethel; then Ella Fitzgerald is Ethel's choice for the ultimate in lightness, purity, and precision. In fact, the Marco Polo in Vancouver advertised Ethel as "Ethel Ennis, A Singer to Rival Ella Fitzgerald." *Vancouver Sun* columnist Bob Smith stated, "Interestingly, the last time Ella was in town nearly three years ago, *she* alerted *me* to Miss Ennis." Apparently Ella had been keeping abreast of Ethel's progress. In an interview in *Down Beat* (November 18, 1965), while discussing one of the tunes on an Ennis recording with jazz critic Leonard Feather, Ella warmly endorsed the younger singer, "Yes, she did a fine job on this one. Ethel has a lovely sound and phrases well; she's really one of the best singers coming up."

Smith could not resist bringing the two divas together. He arranged for Ethel to catch a glimpse of Ella's show at the Queen Elizabeth Theater in downtown Vancouver before her own show at the club. Prior to this performance, Ethel had seen Ella one other time: while she was a student at Booker T. Washington Junior High in Baltimore. Ella had performed there and left her mark on young Ethel.

About the Vancouver meeting with Ella, Ethel recalls, "I caught the first part of her show and then went backstage. We acknowledged each other. She exuded almost a motherly instinct and I felt like she took me to her bosom . . . The woman is phenomenal; she really is in a class all by herself."

Back at Purcell's office in New York, things were not so loving. And finally there came the day when it was "the last straw" in the cross-booking situation that Ethel had set up for herself. Powell had booked her into a private country club in Calgary, Alberta. When her plane landed in Canada, Ethel was handed a message that she had a call from Purcell's office in New York to appear with Doc Severinsen at a rodeo in Tennessee. Well, here she was in Canada and this gig had already been promised. She felt that there was nothing she could do about Purcell's booking at the moment, so she turned it down. And basically that was the beginning of the end of Ethel's stint in big time show biz: no show, no biz.

Ethel *did* show at the country club at Calgary, though, and when she arrived she was greeted with a big surprise. When the board members, most of whom were Texans, discovered that Ethel Ennis was black, they had a field day expressing their rage to Powell and members of the band. It was an all out prejudicial picnic, with band members ready to walk off if Ethel were given any trouble. The conversation went round and round for hours. During this time, Ethel was kept out of it, but she got the point nevertheless. Eventually an agreement was reached. Ethel went on and managed to once again melt the barriers of racial discord through the warmth of her talent.

In New York, however, things had gotten more than warm for Ethel; the smoldering had grown into a full-scale flame. Ethel's growing sense of mistrust and low self-esteem began to express themselves. As she tells it, "I had been fooled by the business a few times, so I thought I'd better step aside and learn more about it. I felt like I was a racing car travelin' in the fast lane and lookin' real good, but with no seats, no engine. I thought the business would be the engine—the power. I thought I would have been just for show and would have had to rely on their power for everything else.

"At the time, people were lookin' at my career and I felt that I had to give something back. The audiences were gettin' larger and I wanted not to be shallow. All of the people were lovin' and admirin' me, but inside I knew that there was more of me to love. I felt I wasn't developed enough as a person to match their adoration."

By the end of 1966, Ethel Ennis, who rarely had much say about career matters, took a very strong stand about continuing on in show business. As she remembers it: "Purcell was right about what he knew and I knew what was right for me. I wasn't ready for his seriousness, so I said, 'NO!' It was a definite 'NO!' There wasn't anything wishy-washy about it; it was N . . . O . . . It was very clear!"

Purcell had tried everything he knew at the time to guide Ethel, but as he recalls, "Everytime she was about ready to crack through, she would just as quickly go back in her shell . . . Parts of artists are underdeveloped. Many can't handle success, so they become a big fish in a small pond, and they have a happy personal life. Back then her personal life was chaotic and sometimes we couldn't reach her. Eventually the record company said, 'We don't need this.' We believed in her and we were killing ourselves on her behalf, but she took it for granted that we'd always go out of our way for her. Clearly she wanted her career to play a smaller role and she opted for a happier personal life."

In 1966 all Ethel Ennis wanted from Gerry Purcell was *out*. In his way he had served as a test of her commitment, although she couldn't see it then. So Ethel Ennis canceled out the New York contract. And with that move she also canceled out any strong representation in the show business network, recordings on RCA, and bookings on national television and in clubs that Purcell was connected with. In short, she canceled out the big time; the first and only epoch of Ethel's resistant climb to stardom had come to an end. As Purcell tells it, "I felt that she had this great potential and I got a certain sense of satisfaction in seeing it grow, but the bottom line was that I ended up with a net loss of $20,000."

Meanwhile, Ethel still had Powell, Godfrey, and once in a great while, a "Tonight" show, but basically it was over, finished, kaput. And so was her marriage. The Red Fox in the meantime, was in its declining years, Ethel had developed asthma, and rock 'n roll was raking in the money.

In the best tradition of the Hollywood movies, stars don't usually walk out when they are about ready to break through. But Ethel Ennis created her *own* tradition and that's the way she played it out for herself in her brush with the big time. Ethel was involved in high-level show business for only two and a half years, but the effects were so potent that it would take her nearly the next twenty to get herself clear on what those years were about.

Although she was hesitant to examine the entire episode for a long time, the benefits that she accrued from those years gave her enough to keep her going for a long time, thanks to Purcell. Powell came to her courtesy of her booking at the Slate Brothers Club in Los Angeles; Godfrey came to her courtesy of the booking on Garroway's program; and even an event farther down the road, the singing of the National Anthem at Nixon's second inauguration, came to her courtesy of someone listening to her recordings on RCA—but that's a story for later on. Suffice it to say that Purcell provided fertile territory for Ethel Ennis, but the time just wasn't right for Ethel. For a long while she saw very little value tied in with those years; instead she viewed them with great aloofness and mild resentment. Her answer to the entire business was to board a plane and leave the "devil's den" of show business behind as she returned back home to the deep blue sea of the security of Baltimore and the comfort of the Red Fox.

JAMES J. KRIEGSMAN, NYC

In 1963, Ethel hit the big time when she was discovered by Gerry Purcell *(above)* and consequently signed on as his client. Purcell's management was instrumental in getting her an RCA Victor recording contract and bookings into major niteries throughout the US and abroad. Several months after she signed with him, she appeared in Los Angeles at a hot spot called the Crescendo. Ad at right appeared in *Variety*, March 16, 1964.

The slick ad above is a far cry from the earlier ATCO one. RCA spared no expense when they ran this full page in the trades in order to promote Ethel's first RCA album, *This Is Ethel Ennis* recorded in late 1963.

Once more with feeling: songs by Ethel Ennis

Because everybody's asking for more, here's Ethel Ennis singing and swinging "Once Again." Her first album clearly proclaimed a new vocal star on the scene. Her second again demonstrates an amazing talent on standards like "Love for Sale," "For Every Man There's a Woman" and "Like Love." Get your second helping of Ethel Ennis—today!

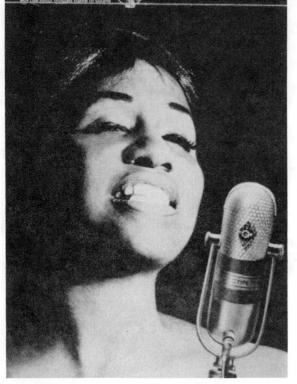

Another example of the differ ence between small time and bi time. This beautifully designe ad prepared by Grey Advertisin Inc., was run in major publica tions, this time to promote th second RCA album, *Once Again Ethel Ennis. Esquire* feature this ad in their July, 1964 issue

Red Levitt leads his orchestra; Ethel Ennis sings solo at jazz festival. Other pictures on page 3

State Opens 4th of July Celebration

Youth Returns in Force; 11,000 at Jazz Festival

MICHAEL J. R. KELLY

During the same month, July, 1964, Ethel amazed crowd and critics in her stunning performance at the Newport Jazz Festival as evidenced by her photo on the front page of *Providence Journal (above)*. RCA immediately rushed into production with album number three, *Eyes For You*. Photo at right is ad-mat used by record dealers to promote the album in local newspapers.

THE WORD'S OUT –

ETHEL'S "IN"

eyes for you/ethel ennis

Another top album from Ethel Ennis, the most talked-about singer on the scene today. "The Song Is You," 11 others.

NEW on RCA VICTOR

DEALER IMPRINT

For Ethel the greatest ever!

ETHEL ENNIS
DAVID FISHER
extra added attraction
ROBERT COLE TRIO

THE *LIVING ROOM*

Cocktails & Supper from 5 p.m.-7 Days
915 2nd Ave. (49 St.) EL 5-2262

From East Coast . . .
In 1965, Ethel became a regular on Arthur Godfrey's radio program. She spent several days a week taping in New York *(above)*. Often she combined tapings with appearances in night spots in New York City like the Living Room *(left)*.

. . . To West Coast

n Fall of '65, Ethel appeared at a
zz festival, in Monterey *(above)*.
his time no one was surprised
bout her talent as they had been
t Newport. Critics were beginning
o say things like, ". . . one hopes
ne promise will be fulfilled before
oo long."

 marquee arises out of the Las
egas desert *(right)* announcing
ne headliners at the Fremont
lotel. This shot was taken by
thel during her time there in
)ecember, 1965.

ETHEL ENNIS, nightly

DAVID HIS

Another red hot hom base, was the Red Onic in Aspen, Colorado, oi of Ethel's favorite plac to perform. The love affa was mutual. Ads placed i the *Aspen News* (*top ar opposite, bottom*) captu the mood of Ethel's pe formances. Joe Kloess, ke boardist in ad above now Dionne Warwick man on the ivories.

Musicians at the Re Onion Joe Kloess (*fro row*) Paul Warburton (*lef and Mike Buono (*rigi rear*) and Ethel take tim out to enjoy the beauty the Rockies (*left*). The en of 1966, was also the en of Ethel's business rel tionship with Gerry Pu cell. She plays her la booking through hii (*opposite, top*) at a count club in Rhode Island.

Ethel is back!

Ethel Ennis Nightly

Red Onion

After two and a half years in the big time, Ethel had had enough. She decided that the way they ran business wasn't the way she wanted to do things. So she cut her ties with Purcell and came home to Baltimore. The pained look on her face as she sings (*above*) may have been a reflection of her state of inner turmoil at that time.

VII   *Everything Must Change*

*E*THEL ENNIS returned home to Baltimore. Admirers were glad she was home again, yet they also harbored unspoken feelings of disappointment. The doors to that glorious kingdom of show business had been opened for their object of adoration and what did she do? *She*, the chosen one, had turned on her heel, slammed the door shut, and walked *out—that's* what she did. Unthinkable! Local star-worshippers were dumbfounded and confused. They wanted to know, "Why, Ethel? Why did you do it? We believed in you." Once again the answers were not simple.

Does anyone know for sure *why* we do *what* we do? Suppose we lived life without the gratification of instant answers all of the time and focused instead on the possibility of what life *can* be? Perhaps there is more value in creating our lives with the sense of openness, aliveness, and adventure of an explorer, one who asks, "What does it take to bring forth fully into the world the promise of who I am as a human being? What difference could the knowing of *this* contribute to the evolution of that experiment which we call human *being*?"

Assuredly back in 1966, Ethel was not consciously asking herself these kinds of questions; instead she was operating on instinctive feelings of survival and self-preservation. In all fairness to Ethel, it must be acknowledged that she did attempt in her way to play the game, but she just wasn't ready or willing to meet the demands of the business. She was lacking the awareness, wisdom, and confidence that would eventually be hers with the passing of the years. Ethel instinctively sensed this lack, this something missing. She clearly felt that if she remained, the industry would have gobbled her up alive.

However, this assumed myth of self-destruction (after all, look at Billie Holiday, Elvis Presley, Marilyn Monroe, Judy Garland, Janis Joplin) is not the way it *has* to be. There are plenty of "little people" in all walks of life where the demands of living are seemingly just as intense for far less reward. People can "make it" or self-destruct at any level, there is simply more publicity when that person is a "name." The common thread among those who are hell-bent on self-destruction appears to be, strangely and unbeknown to themselves, *a fear of success.*

In her book, *Overcoming Fear of Success* (Warner Books, 1982), Dr. Martha Friedman explains:

> . . . success . . . is not defined in terms of fortune . . . fame . . . power . . . prestige . . . possessions (although it may include these externals, all icing on the cake). I am talking about *internal success,* the lack of which makes external success, although perhaps fleetingly fulfilling, certainly in the final analysis painfully hollow.
>
> The sort of success I mean consists of . . . getting to do what you really want to do in your work life and in your love life, doing it very well, and feeling good about yourself doing it. The fear of success is *not* getting what you really want because you unconsciously feel you don't deserve it.

By the time Ethel returned home to Baltimore, she had already spent more than half of her thirty-four years in the business. She had traveled the entire road—from small night clubs in East Baltimore, to major jazz festivals, to luxury rooms both here and abroad. She had been involved in recording contracts, TV appearances, and a major international tour. She had received her fair share of critical acclaim and a heavy dose of press coverage as a personality. She had met and talked with the great and the famous and in some circles was ranked among them. Not bad for a naive little black girl from the projects in Baltimore, one who insists that she never wanted to be a star.

But Ethel's Daddy remembers a different tune. He recalls a demure and ladylike little girl who quietly whispered one day, barely loud enough to be heard, "When I grow up, I want to be a star." Grown-up Ethel doesn't remember ever uttering those words. In her view it all just kind of "happened" as if by chance—by accident. There are those who believe life happens by accident, and there are others who believe that nothing happens by accident, that everything in life happens on purpose and that we ourselves are the cause of what happens. However one looks at it, it is clear that a distinct pattern was going on in Ethel's career. The *right* people seemed to magically show up at the *right* time to guide her in the *right* direction toward her next *right* step on the road.

Time and again the pattern repeated itself. Time and again the people involved seemed to be attracted to the paradox before them: a great natural warmth and talent who should have been but wasn't yet a "big star." This was true of George Fox, Ray Fox, Gerry Purcell, and John Powell. In another sense this was also true of Shery Baker, Benny Goodman, Andy Wiswell, and Arthur Godfrey. They were all men. They were all white. And they were all dedicated to Ethel as a talent and in varying degrees, as a person. They all seemed attracted to Ethel and she to them. This turn of events served her in good stead during those days when America was dominated by white male supremacy.

On a very basic level, these "great white fathers" (and brothers, depending on their age) made it possible for a young black female artist to enter worlds that would have been barred to her otherwise. On another level, their presence in Ethel's life clearly was no accident. In retrospect it is easy to see that Ethel Ennis was gathering the seeds of awareness needed for her own growth so that she could shape the purpose for her life and art. That purpose—the building of a bridge of understanding and acceptance between all peoples through the power of her music—has become her *raison d'être.*

In the same way that an anthropologist needs to go out in the field to study another people before he can clearly share his findings with his own, so it was with Ethel Ennis and the white culture. Before she could come home again to her own people and share with them her discovery that *all* people—white, black, yellow, red, or blue; disabled or able-bodied; gay or straight; rich or poor; famous or unknown—at their very essence possess the same God-given promise of being, she needed to go out in the world and do her research. Her great white fathers and brothers were the guides who gave her access to those worlds.

By 1967 the first part of the basic field work had been done. It was time to come out of the field and into the inner world of self. In musical parlance, it was time to "woodshed," to go inward and create anew before going out again. Until now Ethel's life had moved so quickly that somehow she had missed out on getting to know who *she* was and what *she* wanted. She had literally put her life in the hands of her managers and depended on them to tell her what to do next, and sometimes when they did, it wasn't what she wanted anyway. It was now time for Ethel Ennis to discover for herself what it was she really wanted and then to learn to express these wants in a way that could accomplish her purpose. So Ethel made this commitment to herself. The road to external success would become less traveled for a while.

As Ethel began to slow down the pace, she still continued to play a steady round of gigs, mostly on the West Coast. In between, she commuted to New York several days a week to tape the Godfrey program, which she did until it ended in the spring of 1973. The seven albums that she had recorded between 1955 to 1965 were floating around out there somewhere in the marketplace. There were some changes, too. Ethel began moving toward a more contemporary sound with pop tunes like "Ode to Billy Joe" and "Sneakin' Up On You"; and when she performed, she had blossomed into a full-fledged, stand-up vocalist. She left the piano playing to her keyboardist, who was usually joined by bass and drums to complete the rhythm section. That is, everywhere but at the Red Fox, where tradition, the budget, and availability of capable piano players caused Ethel to revert to form and play for herself.

Life at the corner of Pennsylvania and Fulton had changed since those freewheeling early days in 1955. The mood of anger that had started in Watts was beginning to find its expression in Baltimore. The patrons of the Red Fox felt its effects. By 1967 the area had changed dramatically. As Ethel recalls it, "The patrons became victims of robberies and purse snatchings. The kids on the street would cut the pockets out of people's pants. Sometimes customers would walk in with their heads smashed. I'm tellin' you, it really got bad around there. So people started stayin' away. The flower had died. It bloomed. It was beautiful. And it died."

Shortly before the final demise of the Red Fox, George Fox asked Ethel if she would come back to perform to "give the room a shot in the arm." She agreed. During this period, while she was at home one spring day, Ethel received a phone call. It was from a young reporter with the Baltimore *Sunpapers*. He had seen Ethel perform at the Red Fox in 1963 while he was stationed at the Army Intelligence School at Fort Holabird. In the interim, he went to Germany where he finished out his tour of duty and was now back in Baltimore working the police beat and writing an occasional feature or two. One night after he finished the midnight shift, he wandered into the club to relax with some music and a beer. He was amazed to see that Ethel Ennis was still performing there. "Why," he thought, "does this marvelous singer continue to perform in a funny little place like this?" Of course, he had no idea of where Ethel had been during the intervening years. He only knew that she was there when he left and she was still there when he returned.

Like the others, Earl Arnett was curious. The paradox of "so much talent and so little recognition" led to some questions. So he decided to call her for an interview. She agreed, and they started the interview—which stretched into several days, and then into several weeks. That was in March.

Earl began to spend more time around Ethel and her gang. Right away, as Ethel says, "The love bug was in the air." At the time, Earl was dating a young lady who lived in New York. It wasn't long before he brought her to the club to hear Ethel. Betsy noticed the vibes between them and got the message. She gracefully backed out of the picture. Earl, in the meantime, became intrigued with the Ethel phenomenon. There was always a question mark encircling the air around Ethel. "Where has she been *hiding*?" "Why haven't I heard about *her* before?" Earl says that people felt like they were participating in an "in" kind of experience when they were around Ethel and her music.

The lady certainly wove her magic around the serious-minded young reporter. During the five months of their courtship, they had only one official "date"—the standard kind where the gentleman invites the lady to dinner. Breakfast after the show was more their speed. As Ethel tells it, "One night after I finished at the Red Fox, a group of friends were planning to go out for early breakfast after the show on 'The Avenue.' They were makin' all these plans and I turned back and hollered at Earl, 'Hey, do you wanna come along?' He accepted, and I decided to ride over with him. Well, he was driving this old green Nash Ambassador that wouldn't go in reverse, and he would have had to go around the block to make it go in the right direction, so I got this good idea. I jumped out—he stayed in the car behind the wheel—and I was pushin' and pushin' the car to go in the other direction."

And thus started the pattern of the relationship between E 'n E (as they call themselves). Earl sat in the driver's seat with his hands on the wheel, but it was Ethel who was doing all of the pushing—usually in the wrong direction, and especially away from getting anywhere too fast. (On this point, Ethel will argue: "Why do you have to move so fast? Whenever you get there, it'll be on time.")

With Earl, Ethel not only blew her ladylike image, she broke every existing pattern that she had established with the other men in her life. It's true that Earl also was white, and Earl also just *happened* to show up where she was performing and became entranced with her talent. But Earl Arnett did not offer Ethel Ennis any contract, any promises of fame and fortune, any entree into the world of show business. In fact, he makes a point of stating that he didn't care about and wasn't interested in the entertainment business, not in the least. So right from the start they were perfectly matched: Ethel didn't want to remember it and Earl knew nothing about it to forget.

Earl brought to the relationship an intense curiosity about life and people that had been kindled and fed by his adventures as a member of a globe-trotting military family. He was born in a small town in Indiana, and by the time he met Ethel, he had been educated in schools in America, Austria, and Japan. He did most of his military service in Germany, where he stayed for six months after he was discharged, shuttling back and forth between Munich and parts of Austria. He soaked up a lot about European culture, those kinds of things that would appeal to his serious intellectual bent. (He majored in philosophy and history.) But one aspect of life that he apparently didn't pursue was the nightlife. On this Miss Ennis was the expert.

Although she detested the world of show business and what it came to represent in her mind, at home, like it or not, Miss Ethel was "Miss Show Biz of Baltimore." After all, how many people in her town had been where she had? The mystique was there and it was like a magnet. People were attracted to it and wanted to be near it. Ethel, being a warm-hearted soul and a lover of fun besides, didn't do anything to turn anyone away. So sometimes after work at the club, people would drop by the house on Leighton Avenue. To Earl it looked like a living re-creation of the cast of characters from Ethel's tune "Nightclub." They were all there in the living room, "the jazzy and the pseudo-hip folks . . . the slightly gay and wide-eyed teen . . ." and maybe every once in a while a "junkie" or two. No matter, Ethel loved them all.

It was party time! When Earl tells the story, he makes a strong point to include the fact that while this colorful cast of characters had gathered around Ethel, she herself maintained her shy, ladylike persona, and above all, she did not partake of the smoke or drink. So in the midst of what Earl calls this "chaotic" scene, Miss Ethel held court. Earl, on the other hand, understood nothing about these "nightlife folks," so one night he got irritated and took his bookish self out of there. He left. Good-bye.

Ethel wasn't going to let what looked like a good thing get away that easily. So at five a.m., after the party folks cleared out, Miss Ennis (who these days rarely drives herself anywhere), got into her car and headed down to the apartment on Bolton Street to retrieve her treasure, Earl "The Pearl"—and that was the end of heavy-duty partying on Leighton for a while.

Right before they met, there were signs that Ethel Ennis was ripe for a new relationship. Exactly four days before Earl appeared in Ethel's life, while she was on a gig in Boston, she first started telling the press about her domestic side. She told them about her love for cooking and her penchant for making bread. This theme would come up again, not only because it was true, but because it symbolized another role in Ethel's life:

that of the nurturing provider. As she said in *The Patriot Ledger* (March 24, 1967), "And can I make bread, 'specially light bread. I get so carried away making bread sometimes I have to give it to the neighbors. For a while, I was trying to find people I hadn't given bread to."

At last Ethel knew exactly what she wanted. With the same certainty that she knew that she wanted *out* of show business, she knew she wanted *in* to marriage with Earl Arnett. "I didn't have to hem and haw. I felt that here was the person I prayed for. I always wanted someone priestlike, quiet. Someone with gentle strength. Not a macho or a boaster. A person who knew who he was and what he wanted to do."

Careerwise, Earl knew that what he wanted to do was to become a feature writer for the *Sun*. During the interim between the change from police reporter to feature writer, he took some time off and was free to travel with Ethel. The first trip was fairly routine, a visit to New York while Ethel was on a regular gig taping the Godfrey program. But as it was the first of many trips they would take together, it was also the fulfillment of another of Miss Rose's predictions. Soon after this little jaunt, Ethel had to leave the "love nest" again for a trip to the West Coast to perform in Spokane and Los Angeles. The plane was leaving from Dulles and Earl offered to drive Ethel to the airport. When they checked in, Ethel found that she had to take a shuttle from the terminal out to the airfield. Earl wasn't ready to leave her at that point, so he rode with her out to the plane. As Ethel tells it, "There we were on this little bus and he's kissin' me and kissin' me. And I thought, 'Oh my, I don't know what to do about this.' I mean, I was never the affectionate one; it was Earl who was affectionate. And here we were—I'm black and he's white and we're in Virginia yet . . . Anyhow, I thought about that all the way across the country. I thought, 'This guy is really *serious.*'"

Ethel went on to Spokane and gradually adopted that city as her "home base" on the West Coast. During this period, she began to open herself up more to her audiences. She felt that there was more of a give and take developing.

Ethel says, "I had more spontaneous freedom in my work. I might be coming up to a word in a song, and I could do it *this* way. The next night I might come up to the same word and do it *that* way. There was more flexibility in the moment, depending on whatever I felt. It was different than having to do it the same way all the time, like when you have an act. I just did *me* and people liked it."

When Ethel finished the gig in Spokane, she flew down to Los Angeles for a month-long stint in the Hong Kong Bar at the Century Plaza. When she got off the plane, there was a surprise waiting. As Ethel tells it, "Who's waitin' for me in L.A. but Earl? I figured, 'Now this cat is really serious, he came all the way cross country.' It was like he was sayin', 'Here I am an open book, read me.' I felt it was time for me to try to match his energy."

By this time it was May. They had known each other barely over a month. During Ethel's gig, they set up housekeeping on Sunset Boulevard in the Sunset Doheney Motel. Almost immediately, Ethel took over the care and handling of Earl Arnett. First off, she wanted to add a dash of more style. As she says, "You know how some newspapermen look; they don't pay attention to what they wear. He always used to wear these loose baggy trousers. I called them parachute pants. So I got an idea: I wanted to take him shopping and buy him a new wardrobe."

Earl resisted. He felt uncomfortable about letting Ethel spend the money on him, and he wasn't very much interested in clothes one way or the other. As Earl says, "Ethel wanted to fix me up, to have me look more presentable." Ethel Ennis had now taken the role in Earl's life that she had resisted Gerry Purcell taking in her own. Ethel didn't want anyone to tell her what to do, but it was perfectly OK with her to tell someone else what to do. As she says, though, "I wasn't asking him to do anything that would hurt him."

However this wasn't entirely accurate. After they "frocked out" on their shopping spree in outlet stores and haberdasheries, Earl ended up with the beginnings of a new wardrobe. It was a nice wardrobe as Ethel recalls. In fact the clothes are still there in the closet. "We bought this double-breasted black sport jacket, a pair of black dressy loafers, and two grey shirts with deep collars, both the same. And I loved the pants. I always felt that Earl hid his physique. So I wanted him to get a pair of tight pants. Well he did. They were also a beautiful shade of grey.

"But he wasn't used to wearing tight pants after wearing the baggy ones for so long. A few days later he developed a rash and we had to get some powder to fix him up."

Not to be outdone by her new-found role as a fashion consultant, Ethel's musical energy also took a quantum leap. While they were out west, the Los Angeles Times (May 5, 1967) said: "Possibly her greatest asset is an adroit vocal maneuvering or finesse that also distinguished such popular music giants as Ella Fitzgerald, Sarah Vaughan, and Peggy Lee. Connoisseurs of American jazz have noted this for some time. Now Miss Ennis is in a position to display it full blown to the general public." Variety also (May, 1967) had good things to say: "Miss Ennis is an outstanding chirper whose versatile pipes and styling roam [a] wide spectrum . . . Result is near perfection."

Of the "giants" mentioned above, Ella and Peggy Lee have already been alluded to. And then there was Sarah. Ethel doesn't remember which festival it was, Newport or Monterey, but somewhere in her memory she recalls an evening of watching Sarah perform. If Ella is lightness, purity, and precision, and Peggy Lee is sensuality, then Sarah gets Ethel's vote for the ultimate in technical virtuosity—and more. As Ethel recalls, "I remember seeing Sarah. It was a perfect evening under the stars. Everything was perfect—the sound, Sarah—everything. She was singing 'Maria' and it was almost like time stopped. All you could hear was the beautiful voice. All became One. It was my first experience of being mesmerized by a voice."

In the meantime, Earl continued to be mesmerized by Ethel. He returned to Baltimore in June to take on his new job as a feature writer. He left Ethel on the coast and came back home to his apartment on Bolton Street. By the time Ethel returned, they both knew that this was *it*.

Shortly thereafter, Earl took up temporary residence with Ethel. By now Ethel had developed some business sense and offered Earl a deal. "He was spending a lot of time at the house and he still had his apartment on Bolton Street. I thought it would be sensible and economical for him to be living here, and it didn't feel right to live together unmarried, so I suggested that we get married.

"Earl was rather reluctant. He promised himself he wouldn't marry till he was forty. [He was twenty-six at the time, eight years younger than Ethel.] He thought he would have to give up some of his freedom, but that wasn't so."

In August, they flew out to Aspen, Colorado where Ethel was appearing in a jazz festival at her favorite spot, the Red Onion. There in the beauty of the Rockies on August 29, 1967, Earl and Ethel went to the courthouse accompanied by club owner Werner Kuster, who gave the bride away; pianist Joe Kloess (now Dionne Warwick's keyboardist), who was the best man; and the drummer and bass player, who were witnesses. There Ethel Ennis became Mrs. Earl Arnett. And to complete the experience, Earl's wedding attire consisted of the double-breasted black jacket and the loafers that Ethel had given him during their time together in Los Angeles. He also wore the tight gray pants.

After lots of well wishes and gifts from fans and fellow musicians, the couple was off to the next gig. Once again, Ethel headed for Spokane. And now Earl, too, began to share some of the limelight. The *Spokesman Review* (September 6, 1967) preserved the event as columnist Thomas Goldwaithe reported that Ethel ". . . was especially merry because she's on her honeymoon." After he declared, "If you want to see one of the best club singers in the business, there she is," he went to their table between shows to interview them. Ethel assured reporter Goldwaithe that married life wouldn't interfere with her career. Earl "nodded enthusiastically."

Earl had been advised from the beginning that he shouldn't be involved in her career. He was warned that it was not good practice to be a wife's manager. He said recently, "My kind of personality didn't fit show business. For Ethel's career, I was the wrong person for her to end up with. Her marriage to me was not a step forward in those terms. But as a person for her personal happiness, that's another matter."

When they met, as Earl recalls, "Her life was somewhat complicated. It was a life I was unfamiliar with. Her daily affairs were all jumbled up, in contrast to mine." So Earl helped her to organize her finances and attempted to help her untangle some of the confusion. Until that time, Purcell's office had kept Ethel's finances straight; now Earl took over.

During the first year of their marriage, they got a loan to buy back Purcell's contract. They went to New York and hired an attorney, paid the price, and declared Ethel a free agent.

They also had to confront their parents with their interracial marriage. On Ethel's side, as Earl recalls, "Ethel's mother looked at it askance. She was primarily interested in money and the career. So she said, 'If you're going to marry a white man, why not marry a rich one?'" Andrew, Sr., on the other hand, was more open-minded about it. His attitude was, "As long as she's happy, it's all right with me."

On the Arnett side of the family, the issue was a bit more traumatic. Earl stopped off in Arizona, the family home, on his way back from their honeymoon. Ethel had remained behind to do a taping. Earl broached the issue. It was a terribly painful moment. As Earl explains, "I asked them, 'What would you think if I got married to a black woman?' I figured that with all of the experience that they had in Army life, with their democratic outlook, and the various mixtures of people we had lived with, they would value a person strictly for their abilities and talents."

But that wasn't what happened. Earl was taken aback. "They were concerned and that was surprising to me. My father felt that he had not gained a daughter, but that he had lost a son. He held that position for nine years. My mother was more concerned about our relationship as father and son. She was concerned for my own welfare, and she had some serious fundamental questions about a black and white marriage. It wasn't until nine years later that it was all resolved and Ethel and I were free to take the trip together to Arizona to meet the family."

During those days interracial marriages carried a heavy handle: miscegenation. The word even sounded like some disease. And it was illegal in the state of Maryland until just a few months after the Arnetts got married. Not that it would have made any difference to them. In their quiet and subtle ways, they both rebelled against society if they felt that their views were right. In many respects it took an act of courage to go through with the marriage knowing that they would risk the disapproval of others around them. But Earl and Ethel never were bothered too much by that kind of thinking. As Ethel says, "The Spirit doesn't have any color."

And so with business contracts out of the way and parental opinion fully expressed, the Arnetts settled down to build their life together. Earl took care of the basic necessities, which gave Ethel a free choice about which gigs she wanted to do. Sometimes he made suggestions about musical matters and always he was there to support and encourage. But at this time, Earl was interested in pursuing his own career at the newspaper.

Ethel began to expand in new directions, both inwardly as a human being and artistically as a musician. In 1970 she returned to Switzerland and performed in the Hazy Land chain in Zurich (downstairs from the concert hall where she had performed with Goodman in '58) and in Basel. While she was there, she was told by an actress, the wife of one of the club's owners, "You've got to dazzle them from the minute you walk out on stage, *before* you even open your mouth. After that, people should be sitting on the edge of their seats waiting for the next moment. And that's *just the beginning*; it's got to go *up* from there. Sure, it helps if you can sing, but even if you can't, well, you've still made some kind of impression."

No matter where she went, even in Switzerland, Ethel couldn't escape the voice of show biz. This time she began to listen.

Back in Baltimore in 1970, it wasn't the voice of show biz that was resounding throughout the town; it was another voice that caught the ear of everyone: urban renewal. The city was coming back to life, waking up from a long, sleepy history. Earl as a reporter was very attuned to what was happening around him, a gift he passed on to Ethel. As the downtown area began to come to life, a group of spirited visionaries thought it would be fitting to celebrate the city, its renaissance, and its neighborhoods. They called their dream "the City Fair."

On September 26, 1970, at the first City Fair, Ethel Ennis made her debut as the city's leading artist-in-residence. A group of people, 10,000 strong, gathered at Hopkins Plaza to see and hear Baltimore's own "Queen of Jazz." Ethel says, 'We headlined the fair on Saturday night. I sang with the US Army Studio Band and used the arrangements from my recordings. It was a great experience. There were people from all walks of life lovin' one another and enjoyin' the city together.

"My participation was really well received. This was where I started to get Baltimore acclaim, wider recognition in Baltimore. It was the beginning of my relationship with the city. I really have Earl to thank. He encouraged me."

During this period Ethel continued to appear on the Godfrey program. Over the years, she had developed a substantial listening audience. While her fans loved to hear her on the air, they were frustrated by the fact that there was nowhere to buy any of her recordings. Apparently, the albums that were out there were few and far between and difficult to find. It had been six years since Ethel cut a recording. In April, 1971, one of her fans wrote a letter that summed up where Ethel's career was at that time. The ardent admirer stated, "For some time I have wondered whether you do this as a sort of 'thing' with Godfrey or whether you are a regular recording artist. If so, get a new manager, agent . . . and get yourself where people can appreciate the sound!" Ethel, who hates to write letters, never responded.

By September Ethel was the featured headliner again at the second City Fair. This time she rounded up eighteen of the best musicians she could find in the area. The concert was sponsored by the National Brewing Company and included a variety of styles, everything from jazz to pop to rock to country-western. The *Sunpapers* called it a "first." Undoubtedly this was Earl's influence. He is perennially fascinated with how many "firsts" he and Ethel have established in the city, state, country, and world.

Toward the end of 1971, life had slowed down to a comfortable pace. There was a brief stint at the Playboy Penthouse, which had a fairly short life in Baltimore, and a half-hour TV special with guitarist Charlie Byrd called "It's Christmas." But basically it was one of those periods that was like a lull in the conversation, a kind of pregnant pause in the flow of life that seemed to suggest that something big was about ready to burst on the scene.

VIII   *Oh Say, Can You See?*

I T was the first Sunday morning of the New Year in 1972. As Baltimoreans yawned and leisurely perused their Sunday papers, they were greeted by a full color shot of "Singer Ethel Ennis" on the cover of the *Sun Magazine* section (January 2, 1972). Paul Hutchins, staff photographer, captured a portrait of a woman who could have been, from all appearances, a richly endowed society lady as easily as a show biz personality.

There Ethel stood in regal profile. Small spotlights illuminated her ample facial features while diamonds on her fingers and sequins on her gown caught the reflection from the lights and sparkled and glittered against the dark background. To further support the illusion of wealth and glamour, the cover caption reads, "Now she commands $1,000 to $2,000 a week in nightclubs."

That was the cover. On the inside, the headline of the article, a quote from Ethel, didn't quite jive with the outside image: "To Make It You Have To Give Up So Much." Clearly Ethel's opinion of the entertainment world was that it was one of great sacrifice. Since she had returned home from the "field," she began filling in the local press with the news of her discoveries while she was in the big time, and Ethel's news was not good. In 1968 she told *Evening Sun* reporter Josephine Novak (October 11, 1968), "I can't stand the phase of show business that changes you into a package to fit the trend . . . It's all so different from the way I am, and trying to do it was tearing me apart . . . I love the slow quiet things, nothing that would get in your way . . . It takes longer my way, maybe, but. . . ."

During this period Earl and Ethel had begun to evolve a particular position on the issues of fame, fortune, wealth, and stardom. Their attitude was in distinct contradiction to what most people dream of. In fact, they had almost developed a reverse approach to life in their effort to appear unpretentious and unassuming. In some ways, it worked against them; any pendulum that swings too far in the opposite direction can produce a pretense of another kind. At the time that Ethel began making these statements publicly, her mind was still clouded with confusion from the past.

Again in the *Sun Magazine* article she told columnist Jack Dawson, "There are so many demands. They don't bother to nurse you along . . . They put you in a certain category and there you are. That's against my personality."

Ethel was telling the truth; it *was* against her personality. In fact anything that anyone ever suggested that was not Ethel's own idea at the time was against her personality. The problem was that Ethel rarely had a better suggestion in those days. So it went round and round. Ethel was, to put it pointedly, *stubborn*. This is a trait she says that she inherited from her father.

In line with her love of the slow, quiet things, Ethel began to develop her "stay at home" philosophy. She and Earl had gotten the idea that since Ethel didn't like the hassle of being on the road, perhaps the music industry would come to them. In 1972 they were in the midst of trying out this new approach. They involved themselves in a recording project with a New York songwriter who had achieved about the same level of recognition as Ethel. Her name was Gladys Shelley, and she had learned of Ethel's talent through listening to the Godfrey show.

As soon as Ethel discovered that Gladys was a fellow Sagittarian, she took this as a good sign. The two ladies agreed to collaborate. Ethel supplied the voice and Gladys supplied the tunes and the money. And to top it all off, "Mr. I Don't Care About Show Biz," Earl Arnett, stepped in and handled some of the logistics and the details. In fact, the couple formed their own partnership, ENE Productions.

Within several months they completed the first phase of the project, a 45 rpm called, "Does It Hurt to Love." The arrangement was done by Dave Wolpe, who had worked with Ethel on the City Fair concerts. The recording studios were Baltimore-based as well. On the back burner, they had plans for an album called *Ten Sides of Ethel Ennis*. It was to be a privately financed effort, a trend that was becoming more widespread as artists vied for more independent control of their work.

During this time Ethel had learned to play the guitar and began using it in her on-stage performances. She also began to seriously listen to her own recordings for the first time and in doing so made an interesting discovery. As she told Jack Dawson, "My vibrato has widened somewhat. It's more mellow . . . I hope it's improved. I used to hate myself because I sounded so sweet and angelic." This was an odd statement coming from the singer who used to be referred to as "the black Doris Day" and who acknowledges that lady as the ultimate in sweetness and clarity.

Dawson's New Year's article concluded with a revealing statement from the reluctant semi-star: "But sometimes I think I'd like to make it big, if only for my friends, for all the people who had faith in me. You know what I'd like to do is reach that peak and then say, 'Look I've done it. Now let me go back to baking my bread.'"

Shortly after that statement, Ethel was in her kitchen, baking her bread, her hands covered with dough, when the telephone rang. It was almost like deja vu. Just as Ethel thought someone was playing a joke when Billie Holiday called years before, she had the same thought on this occasion. The caller on the other end of the line wanted to know if she could take a few minutes to speak to the assistant to the Vice President. "Vice President of what?," Ethel wanted to know. "The Vice President of the United States," came the reply. Ethel handed the phone to Earl. She didn't have time for ridiculous jokes. But it was no joke.

It turned out that Spiro Agnew had been an Ennis fan for years and was delighted to discover that they were both Marylanders. He wanted to know if she would like to entertain at the State Governor's Ball on the same bill with Danny Thomas and Frank Sinatra. Ethel accepted. She also had a request. She asked that Shery Baker, who in the intervening years had become her hairdresser, be invited as well. The Vice President complied with her request.

After the main festivities of the evening were over, Agnew invited Ethel, Earl, and Shery to his apartment. There Ethel was surprised to see that Agnew had every one of her albums. He also had a piano. So Miss Ennis and the Vice President of the United States played duets together until the early hours of the morning.

That was in January. Shortly after their wonderful evening together, Agnew invited her to sing the National Anthem at the Republican Convention in Florida. Ethel, a registered Democrat, didn't give him the answer immediately. She had some concerns about what the invitation meant. Was she being manipulated for political ends? Was he using her talent and race to further his own gains? After mulling it over with Earl, she concluded that Agnew simply wanted to give her an opportunity because he genuinely was impressed with her talent. So she accepted and the date was set for her to appear in Miami during the convention in the summer of 1972.

Yet even as the machinery was being put in place to renominate Nixon at the convention, and even as Ethel was polishing up her fifty-one piece arrangement of "The Star Spangled Banner" written by David Volpe, five men burglarized the Democratic party national headquarters in the Watergate complex in Washington, D.C. That was on June 17, 1972.

President Nixon immediately denied any White House involvement in the matter. Yet even as he spoke the words, before he was ever renominated or sworn into office for his second term, he knew he was speaking a lie. Subpoenaed tapes released fourteen months later made "one thing perfectly clear": six days after the break-in, Nixon knew of, approved, and directed Watergate cover-up activities.

At the time of the Republican Convention, the scandal had not yet reached its full momentum. So Nixon's cover-up lasted long enough to get him renominated. Ethel Ennis was there to contribute her energy to the celebration, totally unaware, as all of us were, of the turn that Watergate would cause in the life of the country. In the meantime, show business and politics were becoming close partners in stimulating the public psyche.

Talented Miss Ennis, who held that she was apolitical, nevertheless sang the anthem for the Republicans. Ethel says, "We were planning to use the big band arrangement, but the platform where I would be singing, the same one Nixon was speaking from, was so far away from the band—it looked like it was three blocks away—that I couldn't hear them. So the coordinator said, 'Do it without the band. Just sing it!' So that's what I did.

"The response was surprisingly wonderful. I sang it straight then. I didn't go foolin' with it. Later I started thinkin' about it in new ways and started foolin' around with it."

Based on the overwhelming response at the convention, Agnew called again. This time he invited Ethel to sing the anthem at Nixon's inauguration. Now Ethel was getting even more involved with the Republican party. It became a source of confusion for her. Ethel says, "I got in touch with the black leaders in the community to find out what they thought. I had heard so much about the Republicans—that they were out for the rich to get richer and not botherin' about the poor folks. But after thinkin' about it, I thought, 'I'm just gonna sing it for the people.' I was asked, so there must be a reason. It was harder for me this way, with the Republicans, but I love to turn things around. Turn the no's into yes's. I love the challenge. So I said, 'Yes.' "

After Ethel accepted, she started examining the *Star Spangled Banner* again and thinking about our country. This time she wasn't the naive young lady who had represented America in Brussels without even knowing it. This time she knew that this was an opportunity to reach out and touch the heart of the nation.

Ethel earnestly did her homework. As she says, "I started thinkin' about America. It was the time of Vietnam, and America was sick. We were throwin' our sickness onto other countries. I agreed to sing the anthem because I wanted to lullaby America like I was its mother—the mother of America.

"I always wanted to slow down the garbage that was happenin'. I felt that in so many ways progress was killin' us. We go so fast without knowin' the ramifications of the future. America was killin' all of these people. We had been *taught* to kill. The veterans were comin' back all screwed up and shot up. The draft dodgers were tryin' to save themselves, to save their spirit. And the government was tellin' them this was wrong. But they're not knowin' *why*, why they should kill. It wasn't enough of a reason just because the government says its right."

Ethel explored the anthem not only from its philosophical aspects, but its rhythmic ones as well. "The anthem is such a gung-ho song; it's a pub drinkin' song. You can just see them with their beer steins drinkin' their beer and singin'." Ethel breaks into the beat with gusto, imitating the pub crawlers, "Dum-dum-dum-dum-da-dum . . ."

She continues, "The melody has nothin' to do with spirituality at all. We were cryin', 'What's wrong? What's wrong America?' I was tryin' to cradle it and rock it. To comfort and heal it."

By the time the inauguration drew close, Ethel had worked out all of her thoughts about the anthem. She worked it out, not only emotionally, but musically as well. Ethel recalls, "After I started foolin' with it, I worked on the phrase 'land of the free.' That was always the hook in the song for me. I would always hear this expanded note on the word 'free.' I felt that it should be held in a way so people could experience freedom. That was the most important word to me in the anthem. It deserved everything I had to give it."

On Inauguration Day, Saturday, January 20, 1973, Ethel Ennis was ready to sing as she had never sung before. The US Marine Corps Band was on hand to accompany her, but as she prepared to sing, she said, "No, I'll do it alone." The anthem came so late in the program that people had already started to leave. As Ethel began to sing she saw the backs of heads as the crowd moved to disperse. And then the first words, "Oh say can you see" started filling the air. The only sound was the simple, beautifully clear voice. "By the dawn's early light . . ." The crowd stopped moving. "What so proudly we hailed . . ." Their attention was riveted on the attractive black singer at the microphone. From there until the end of the stanza,

Ethel had captured their attention along with that of millions of viewers throughout the country.

Just as the crowd had been stunned nine years earlier at Newport, so were they again on this day in the nation's capital. In remembering her experience of that peak moment in her life, Ethel says, "So many dignitaries said they never heard those words before. They never paid attention. I knew a lot of them were prejudiced, but it surpassed all that. It's reachin' for that commonality in us—it's there if you're alive. It's reachin' past all of the garbage, all of the differences to samenesses. When you connect with that inner power, even if it's just for a second, you'll never be the same. That's when you know there's hope."

Ethel spoke and sang from her heart. For a brief moment the power of her song had unified the nation. People had been reached and touched and soothed by the experience. Mail started pouring into the mailbox on Leighton Avenue from everywhere—the White House, television stations, fans who had gotten her address somehow. They all wanted to know, now in louder voices than ever before: "Where has she been hiding out?" "Why haven't I heard about her before?" "Where can I get a copy of a recording of her singing the National Anthem?" According to the letters on file, people genuinely wanted to locate Ethel or her recordings. As one well-wisher stated in a letter addressed to "Mr. Vice President": "Would it be possible to obtain a copy of that record sung by a beautiful lady at the Inauguration of the President. I was crying. She sang for all of America." Ethel never answered the letters.

Along with her deep emotional outpouring, Ethel's musical pyrotechnics did not go unnoticed. An article in The Sun (January 22, 1973) stated: "Ethel Ennis hit a high F on the word 'free' while singing the national anthem and the note rang throughout the Capitol area with a spirit which must have warmed the coldest heart among the spectators assembled Saturday for the second inauguration of President Nixon and Vice President Agnew. . . ."

The reporter concluded the rather lengthy article (which made the headlines) after describing the hectic madhouse atmosphere of the inaugural ceremonies by stating, "Yesterday as the phone rang continuously with congratulations from friends, messages from her record company in New York and questions from the media, she cleaned out her refrigerator and baked two loaves of bread."

Ethel had done it! And now she could get back to baking her bread. And Earl had done it, too. The front page article was written by Sunpapers feature writer, Earl Arnett. It had taken him six years, but he finally completed his story for The Sun on jazz singer Ethel Ennis. About the inauguration Earl says, "I think Ethel was the first one to sing the National Anthem a cappella up to that time."

The success of Ethel's appearance at the inauguration added some needed fuel for their other project, the new album *Ten Sides of Ethel Ennis.* Gladys Shelley, the tunesmith, had been dubbed "Poetess Laureate of the United States" by "perceptive columnists" according to the liner notes written by Earl Arnett. At the time she lived on upper Fifth Avenue with her chihuahuas and her husband Irving Rosenthal, whom Ethel recalls as "a sweet little short man who owned Palisades Park." The two ladies spent a fortune working out details about the material during long-distance telephone conversations. With production schedules set up in Baltimore and a deal negotiated with a relatively obscure label called Spiral, the project got off to a flying start. However, with Gladys' keen sense of promotion and her New York connections, she soon stumbled onto what appeared to be a better deal. She interested BASF, a German firm known in this country as inventors and producers of magnetic tape, in buying the rights to the master from Spiral. Operating from an office in the Boston area, the company representative from Germany talked with them about the firm's plans for starting a recording label in the US. Earl, who is proficient in German, and BASF personnel negotiated a deal that had all the earmarks of a beautiful opportunity.

BASF was anxious to sign Ethel as their *first* (Earl points out) American artist on their prospective label. Their terms sounded promising: recording dates and performances in Germany and wide-scale promotion in the US. BASF even went so far as to run releases in *Billboard* announcing the signing of Ethel Ennis. But the news was somewhat premature; the deal had not been finalized. And suddenly they were gone. They simply closed up shop and disappeared. One more record deal down the drain. By now botched-up recording deals and Ethel Ennis were an old story.

However, *Ten Sides of Ethel Ennis* was given airplay and distribution here and abroad. And she did receive a royalty check, another first for Ethel.

Meanwhile, Shelley's keen nose for promotion led her to suggest a booking in New York for Ethel. What with the success of the inauguration and her own interests at heart as the songwriter, she located an agent who secured a booking at the Persian Room in the Plaza Hotel for the month of April, 1973. Thus, just as Reba Fox had predicted back in 1955 when she first heard the up-and-coming young singer, Ethel Ennis became "a Persian Room act." Another part of the cycle had been fulfilled.

At about the same time, Godfrey was ready to go off the air. In terms of Ethel's career, this meant a reduction in income. (She received $100 per taping and sometimes taped six shows in two days.) The end of Godfrey's show was also the end of Ethel's last connection with any kind of national media exposure—a heavy price to pay in a market where her name had already faded considerably. New singers and groups were emerging constantly in this fickle world, which by now was totally dominated by rock. Even though the Beatles as a group had split three years earlier in 1970, their legacy, pop explosion number three, had left its irrevocable influence everywhere in popular culture.

But what was this influence? David Tame in his fascinating book, *The Secret Power of Music* (Destiny Books, 1984) addresses just this issue. About rock he states: "Rock, properly understood, is music warfare waged upon an unsuspecting society by guitar-gunners who are frequently fully aware of what they are about . . . It is a global phenomenon; a pounding, destructive beat which is heard from America and Western Europe to Africa and Asia . . . Its 'fans' are addicted, though they know it not, to the 'feelgood' . . . effects of its insistent beat."

Lest rock fans take issue with this reflection on their favorite music, Tame does not single out rock only in this study that cuts through all of human civilization. Earlier he states: ". . . but ultimately all uses of tone and all musical lyrics can be classified according to their spiritual direction, upward or downward . . . To put it plainly, music tends to be of either the darkness or of the light."

Perhaps this, too, was Ethel Ennis' struggle as she attempted to embrace and, at the same time, run away from the commercial music business. Clearly the gift of her voice was her light. But all the rest—the hype, the phoniness, the questionable ethics of the business—was, in Ethel's experience of the entertainment world, just as Honey had always called it, "the devil's den."

So Ethel did her gig at the Persian Room. It was a beginning and an end. Godfrey was there to introduce her on opening night and Spiro Agnew was the guest of honor. Ethel Ennis on that evening was a living demonstration of her unconscious inner spiritual struggle between the lightness and the dark. On the one hand she completed her set of contemporary sounds with one old standard, her in-demand, a cappella rendition of "The Star Spangled Banner." On the other hand, she slipped in a flippant little ditty she had picked up somewhere along the way called "Growing My Own." As the reporter for the *Daily News* (April 4, 1973) stated: "She performed a number that might be a Plaza Hotel first—one dedicated to marijuana indulgers and called 'Growing My Own'." (Earl could chalk up another first.)

There were those who looked the other way on this number, knowing full well that the Vice President of this great country was sitting ringside in the audience. After all, what would this kind of message do to the morals of our country? The *morals* of our country—that line had almost become a bad joke! No sooner had Nixon taken office than five of the seven defendants in the Watergate break-in pleaded guilty. Resignations, firings, and sounds of impeachment echoed throughout the corridors of the White House. In the midst of all this turmoil, almost as if to get the attention off Watergate, Spiro Agnew, the music lover and Ethel Ennis fan extraordinaire, pleaded "no contest" to charges of tax evasion, and he, too, resigned on October 10, 1973. Clearly something was greatly out of whack at the highest levels of government. Ethel intuitively hit the mark when she said, "America was sick."

What role, if any, did popular music have in this growing manifestation of spiritual sickness in our country? Turning back toward ancient wisdom, we discover that in the sixth century BC in China, Confucius knew. As he said in *The Book of Rites*:

> . . . the music of a peaceful and prosperous country is quiet and joyous, and the government is orderly; the music of a country in turmoil shows dissatisfaction and anger, and the government is chaotic; and the music of a destroyed country shows sorrow and remembrance of the past, and the people are distressed. Thus we see music and government are directly connected with one another.

Confucius said it and he knew. It was just as true nearly three thousand years later in 1970s in the US. Pop music was an expression of and a fuel for this spiritually faltering society, a society addicted to power, money, and ego at all costs. The sores were beginning to fester and this manifestation could be heard in the music. In a way it was a good sign; all of this was telling us that we were in a period of great decline, a bottoming out as a world power. It was time to begin turning it around. We didn't have to continue feeding this negative energy. There were those who could see the light, and they began, step by step, to rebuild the spirit of America, starting with themselves from the inside out. Ethel Ennis was one of those people.

In one of the most telling articles written about Ethel, writer Joan Seidman in an interview in the June, 1974, issue of *Baltimore Magazine* captured the shift in Ethel's priorities as a human being. Ethel, now in her early forties, apparently had done some hard work on restructuring the interior of herself, and now the Arnetts were doing some hard work on restructuring the interior of their home. Next they planned to get involved in the community and then the city itself. All of these things they have ultimately done. But the most important aspect of Ethel's growth to be revealed in the article was her love for humanity. For the first time Ethel spoke about "universal love," about her dislike of separatism and her hope for "togetherness." That inner voice of destiny that always seemed to be urging her onward, away from the temporal trappings of the flashy world of show business, came through as well. As Ethel said in the interview with Seidman, "It seems like I always knew where I would be going and that the pace would be slow. But I had the time to bide. It might be a blind way. I might be living in a vacuum—I don't know. But it's a happy one."

And what about success? Did Ethel consider that her life was a success? Perhaps not, if we mean those external trappings, although she had these, too. But success on some deeper level? Well, that was a different story. According to Ethel, "What I'd like to achieve is not for myself. It's for everybody to just have a taste of happiness. Because I do consider myself happy; I think I've reached that. And *that's* successful."

In the same article, Ethel revealed another one of her growing concerns, the children. She said, "That's where you've got to start—with the kids." And she meant it. During that same year, she became involved in what turned out to be an award-winning children's program produced by the Maryland Department of Instructional Television. The program, called "Book, Look, and Listen," entertained thousands of preschoolers into an appreciation for all the various kinds of media they could use for learning. Ethel played a large "klutzy" rabbit whose name was Ethel Earphone. Along with Hector Projector, and J. Worthington Book the Third, Ethel Earphone sang, danced, read stories, showed films, and performed a hundred other feats of magic to get kids excited about learning. And it worked. There were thirty fast-paced, ten-minute segments. It took eighteen months to produce, and Ethel loved every minute of it.

Nineteen seventy-four was also the year that Ethel Ennis and the Baltimore Symphony Orchestra discovered each other and developed a fruitful musical relationship that would continue to grow throughout the years.

In 1975, Ethel did yet another political gig when, as she says, "I continued to get my taste of politics when I performed at a luncheon at the Waldorf Astoria where Henry Kissinger was the speaker." In the meantime, shy and reserved Earl was beginning to get his taste of show biz as he branched out into television. He became a local television personality in his own right as the theater critic on *Critic's Place,* a statewide PBS (Public Broadcasting Service) program. He also had begun participating in many ways in Ethel's career. Show biz was beginning to raise its compelling voice in the quiet and comfort of the Arnett household. But it wasn't the same tinselly voice that had been there all along; this one had the ring of truth in its beckonings.

Then in 1976, as the 200th birthday of the country approached, Ethel was back in New York at work again on another album, this time in honor of the Bicentennial. But it turned out to be a bicentennial bust, another firecracker that fizzled out before it ever got off the ground. There were now at least three of these bummers sitting around in vaults gathering dust. (These were in addition to the other eight that were hither and yon, all over the world, someplace—whereabouts and revenue unknown.) By now it was clear that when it came to Ethel Ennis and recording ventures, there was something about the energy around the projects that seemed to say, "No, Ethel, it won't work. Something that you're doing is not working. It really is time to look at it—if you ever want to cut a successful recording."

So as America put its 200th birthday to bed, Ethel Ennis lulled us to sleep once more with her "Star Spangled" lullaby. This time she sang it on the site of its origin—Fort McHenry in Baltimore.

Ethel Ennis at forty-four had settled down to a comfortable married life with an interested and supportive partner. She had become, as Purcell predicted, "a big fish in a small pond." (Or maybe it's more appropriate to say, a big bird in a small nest, in order to keep the metaphors straight.) She had stretched her wings in new ways and had begun to approach life and the business on her own terms. She and Earl had also discovered that Baltimore was in the throes of a transformation of its own, and there was more than enough room for them to participate and contribute their talents toward the unfolding of Baltimore's fresh and exciting renaissance. Most of all, Ethel seemed to be enjoying the free and easy style of life that she and Earl had created for themselves. There was little else that she seemingly wanted or needed from life at this point. But life never stands still, especially when one begins to take those first faltering steps toward true spiritual awakening.

On August 28, 1967, Ethel Ennis married second husband, *Sun* feature
writer, Earl Arnett in Aspen, Colorado.
Best man Joe Kloess follows the happy
couple as they leave the courthouse
(*above*).

Show business demands never got in
the way of the neighborly chat over the
back fence, especially after Ethel settled
into the leisurely pace of marital bliss
(*right*).

Once Ethel left the big time
she began to participate mor
in Baltimore happenings
Above, with guitarist Charli
Byrd in a publicity shot for
Christmas special on local T\
station, WBAL.

Ethel is flanked by two o
her strongest supporters. O
the left is Shery Baker; friend
hairdresser, and president o
her fan club in the fifties an
on the right, husband, Ear
Arnett. The group is decke
out in their finery for th
Hairdresser's Ball.

Ethel's life began to take on the flavor of the "new" Baltimore that was beginning to emerge during the late sixties and early seventies. Hopkins Plaza,
shown here, became the site for a variety of exciting outdoor events such as
this concert where Ethel was the headliner.

During the early seventies, Eth(
tried new artistic endeavors. Tw
of these are shown here: playin
the guitar and in the backgroun
an Ennis variation on the Jacksc
Pollack approach to painting (lef

In 1972 Earl and Ethel forme
ENE Productions and tried the
hand at producing an album calle
Ten Sides of Ethel Ennis wi
tunes by New York songwrite
Gladys Shelley. They used a Balt
more-based recording studio, Fligl
3 shown here. Ethel can be see
behind the glass (*below*).

One January day in 1972, Ethel received a call from the office of the Vice President of the US. Agnew, a longtime Ennis fan, invited her to perform at the State Governor's Ball in February. On the same bill were Frank Sinatra and Danny Thomas. Agnew speaks while Ethel and Judy Agnew look on.

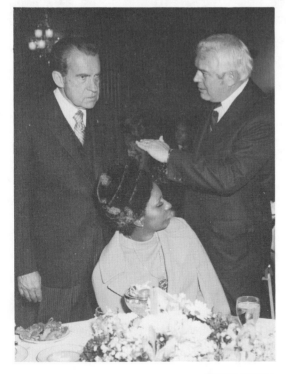

At Nixon's Second Inauguration in January, 1973, Nixon *(above)* congratulates Ethel after her moving a capella version of the "Star Spangled Banner" which brought praise to her from across the nation.

Ethel with Nixon and others at the inaugural luncheon *(left)*.

…el poses with songwriter Gladys …elley at Ethel's opening in the …rsian Room of the Plaza Hotel in …w York City, April, 1973 (*right*). On … heels of Ethel's success at the …uguration and in order to launch the …w album in style, Shelley felt that …h a booking would be ideal. Guest … honor was, by now old friend, Spiro …new (*below*).

In 1974, Ethel took on a new role as Ethel Earph on Maryland State Department of Education's aw winning pre-school program, "Book, Look and List Pictured above Ethel cavorts with buddies: J. Wa ington Book, III and Hector Projector.

Ethel Earphone demonstrates her magical sound for her adoring audience (*left*).

IX

Open Your Eyes
You Can Fly

HE years from 1977 to 1984 could be characterized as a time of reexamination, reconciliation, and rebirth. It was during this period that thousands of us in America and abroad were taking stock of our own spirituality and returning to our roots. We were reclaiming our connection with ourselves, each other, and the universal forces. The New Age, as some refer to it, was just beginning to assert itself. Its underlying truth was a powerful inner experience of returning home. And the home to which we returned was to the true power, the true self, the energy within. It resides in all of us and throughout the whole of the universe. Some call this life-giving, unspeakable force *God*. About this power Ethel Ennis knows much, and whether she addresses it directly in a conversation or not, when one is around her, the loving energy comes through.

Usually the initial spark of this awakening begins with some dramatic life event and so it was with Ethel. In 1977 her past began to break apart when she received news of the death of one of the closest and most loving people in her life. Ethel remembers it well: "I was in L.A. doing a taping session and was talking to Earl on the phone when suddenly for no reason, I felt like the bottom fell out. I was disoriented and started crying and couldn't stop. It was like a veil of sorrow that I couldn't explain. Shortly after that Earl called me back and told me that he had gotten the news that Honey had died.

"After knowing that she had died, I suddenly felt responsible for representing all the things that she had taught me. It was almost like she handed me a baton of spirituality to carry on. I was very clear about that; that's what I was to do from here on out. To live a truthful life. Don't lie to myself. Be the best I can. Work at it. Support it. Respect it. And of course, *be a lady*."

Until this time, Ethel maintained a rather lackadaisical attitude toward her talent. But with Honey's passing, a small spark of the commitment that Ethel had never fully experienced before began to clamor for attention.

As if Ethel needed an extra dose of the same lesson, no sooner had she absorbed the shock of Honey's death then she learned that Mama had developed "a lump on the breast." By this time Bell had already had a stroke, and now she began the arduous rounds of radiation therapy. Two years later, in January, 1979, Bell passed away at the age of sixty-eight.

Even though the relationship between Ethel and Bell was always a struggle for dominance (Ethel can be iron-willed in her own right, so it wasn't only Bell who was attempting to get the upper hand), it was clear from an interview with Bell in 1974, while she and Honey were sharing a home in Glassboro, New Jersey, that she was tremendously proud of her daughter. As reporter Rochine Noto observed: "Record albums were spread all over the dining room table. 'You want to hear my baby?' Mrs. Ennis said excitedly. The phonograph was in a bedroom that was more of a sitting room. It was easy to get lost in the music. 'That's my little girl,' said Mrs. Ennis dreamily." (the *Daily Times*, January 16, 1974)

Of Bell's passing Ethel says, "I feel that Mama's death was a gift that she wanted me to have. I felt that she knew that she didn't want to be a burden for me." Her last days prior to hospitalization Bell spent at Ethel's home. She went into the hospital the day after Christmas in 1978. By early January, she had died.

During the time of Honey's death in 1977, brother Andrew came off the road. He came home to Baltimore to stay after touring extensively with Ray Charles for nine years. His work had taken him all over the globe. While he was traveling, Andy began to have strange experiences. The way he describes it, he began receiving "vibes" from the universe. He felt that he could clearly see into the future. At first he was very frightened; he didn't realize that he too was beginning to get in touch with that powerful inner force. Andy spent long hours sharing these visions with the Arnetts. Ethel was glued to every word. Andy told them that Ethel would meet Muhammed Ali (she *did*, at a benefit at Center Stage in Baltimore); there would be lots of camera trucks parked outside the house with TV cables running into the house (there *were*: since then every local channel has been there to interview Ethel); Earl would be surrounded with piles of paper (he *is*, especially now with his computer print-outs of every aspect of their new business).

Andy returned home at a time when Ethel's life began to shift. He felt that he wanted to be part of what was happening in Ethel's life and in Baltimore. Since his return they have played many gigs together.

For Ethel the late seventies and early eighties were a time of full-blown local acknowledgment from all quarters of the city. Ethel started accumulating awards that recognized her talent, but most especially acknowledged the humanitarianism that she shared with her fellow Baltimoreans. Along with an impressive array of awards from organizations of all kinds, she was nominated to the Hall of Fame of Frederick Douglass High School and was also presented with an honorary Doctor of Fine Arts Degree from the Maryland Institute College of Art. On this particular occasion, Dr. Ethel Ennis still had not yet fully accepted her own worth as a human being. As she says, "When they presented me with the award, I felt that I didn't deserve it. Other people have to work so hard to get that honor. I felt that I didn't do anything to earn it. I wanted to bow my head."

Perhaps Ethel needed to see herself through another's eyes before she could begin to get a deeper sense of who she was. The answer came to her in the form of a powerful photograph, which has since become her trademark. The photograph was taken in November, 1978, one year after Honey's death. Until then, Ethel had used the same head shot that had been taken back in the sixties when she first started working with Powell. She had an aversion to entering a regular commercial studio and simply having a head shot taken. Ethel wanted special attention and she got it: the photographer came to her. Just as Popsie Randolph, the photographer in the recording studio at Capitol, had changed Ethel's life with his lead about the vocalist spot for the Goodman tour, this photographer also changed her life—and Ethel, in return, changed the life of that photographer (who is the author of this book).

The image inspired Ethel to verbalize the feeling she was hit with when Honey died. As Ethel sees it, "The photograph was the beginning of my concept of 'Soft Power.' It was naming the feeling I had in '77. It was powerful, but not harsh. It was light, like something had been lifted. In the photo my eyes are closed; it's my eyes to the inner world. My hands are over my ears; it's very still, very quiet—but there's strength.

"Soft Power is closing your eyes and ears and communicating to and from within. To really listen to that *silent* world; it's not a *verbal* world. It's where you *feel*. And then start feeling *deeper*. And then work from there, from that *inner force*."

When Ethel discovered her inner source of power and coupled it with her growing sense of commitment, she began searching for a way to express her new-found self through her music. She wanted to share the experience with the world-at-large. It was no longer a question of show biz as much as that of self-expression. Ethel's spirit yearned to be back in touch with many people from this whole new level of being. The time had come for the Arnetts to reactivate their company, ENE Productions.

As Earl says, "We had developed a comfortable life, but it wasn't satisfying anymore. I was beginning to feel restricted by my job at the paper and Ethel felt that she wanted to go out and consciously find a bigger audience. Up to that point she felt that it wasn't worthwhile to appear on television programs and to go out in front of large audiences unless she had something to say. At the time she finally felt that she had reached that point."

Early in this emergence from seclusion, they invited a handful of people, mostly artistic types who had worked with them previously, to join them in evolving the company. An interesting conglomeration of personalities and backgrounds formed the core group: a theater director, a fellow musician, an ex-con man in the record business, a marketing-producer type, a set designer, a composer-sound engineer, and a media educator-photographer (the author). At the time very few of the people around the table in the Arnetts' dining room had strong business backgrounds. And Earl and Ethel had only limited experience in working in an intimate capacity with a group, especially one that was looking to them for guidance and direction.

Up to then, the Arnetts had led a relatively cloistered personal life and had not yet learned some fundamental principles about working with a diverse group of people. They sought suggestions from the group and at the same time demanded full control and leadership. But Ethel's ideas had not yet crystallized, so no matter what anyone suggested, it was the wrong thing. People went to great lengths to attempt to support Ethel, just as RCA and Purcell had done in the past, but Ethel herself had no idea of what she wanted. She only knew what she didn't want, and that was nearly anything anyone in the group suggested. Earl, in turn, was very cautious and protective of his Ethel. He perceived that nearly everyone that he had invited as a core group member was in some way trying to take advantage of them.

This negative energy began to manifest itself and finally someone *did* take advantage and ripped them off for several hundred dollars. This deed was done by the ex-con man in the record business, who was known as a "wheeler-dealer." Earl and Ethel felt that by giving him this opportunity, he would begin to change his old "dishonest" ways. He was also unemployed and very hungry. (Everyone in the group was there on a volunteer basis.) Soon after this, Earl sent a letter to the other members of the core group expressing his feelings about the matter. Ethel calls these kinds of letters, "Earl's poison pen letters." An excerpt illustrates the point:

"We take this step with sadness and bitter disappointment since we have always believed in your capacity to overcome the negative aspects of your character . . . We hope that eventually you will learn the necessary lessons required to build a life on human virtues instead of deceptions and lies."

The letter was sent in September, 1980. By November it was clear that the group had served its purpose. All were invited to come together to share their insights, even the "bad guy" who had been admonished by Earl and warned that he no longer had the right to associate with the group. As Earl said in his notes, "Even though Joe [not his real name] had been formally expelled from the group, he was invited because even the criminal's perspective is valuable. After all, we're all sometimes criminals of the heart."

The fact is that while Earl and Ethel were well-meaning and nice people at the time, they also transmitted an arrogant sense of righteousness and a very naive view of what people are all about. In retrospect, it is clear that this early ENE experiment was a testing ground for Earl and Ethel as they started on their road as business people. And while it was a painful experience for some, many valuable lessons were provided that would serve everyone for bigger ventures that lay ahead.

While the group was still together, it did manage to pull off a few basic concerts and an album recorded live at the King of France Tavern in the Maryland Inn located in Annapolis, Maryland. Ethel began working in this fine jazz room in 1973 after her last great New York gig at the Plaza Hotel. After Ethel returned to Baltimore, she began playing some of the clubs around the area. At one of these, the Royal Roost, she discovered a musical partner in guitar player, O'Donel "Butch" Levy. When she went to work at the Inn, she took Levy with her as well as premiere keyboardist Charles "Covey" Covington. This historic tavern was known to have been in existence as early as 1784 and was run by a tavern keeper named Sara Ball. The ambiance provided by the original brick walls and heavy wooden beams created that sense of intimacy that Ethel loved to maintain with her audiences.

So from the steps of the Capitol to the tavern near the waterfront in historic, colonial Annapolis, the presence of American history seemed to be embedding itself in the singer's consciousness. This factor, along with Earl's highly developed historical sense (no doubt dating back to his college history major days), began to impact on Ethel's perceptions and her own sense of involvement as an American artist and an individual in this society.

Musically, the Maryland Inn became a valuable "schoolroom," as Ethel refers to it. Here she began to stretch herself as a performer. As Ethel tells it, "The Maryland Inn became my home base. It was here that I learned how to be more personable—how to read an audience. It was a place for experimenting and refining. I tried more rhythmic things and that was Butch's influence. I tried different instrumentation like guitar and organ. I didn't think I'd like the organ, but Covey is such a sensitive player that it worked out fine. The seventies was the electric sound so I got used to singin' over the electronics. I was discovering the high register and strengthening my voice."

Ethel put these new techniques to work on the album she recorded at the Inn. Simply called *Ethel*, it runs the gamut of selections: blues, jazz, novelty tunes, pop songs, and one number in particular that was a radical departure stylistically and musically from the rest of the album (or anything else Ethel had ever recorded), "Open Your Eyes You Can Fly." Its styling projects an openness and power that had not been demonstrated in the singer's other recordings.

Throughout Ethel's career she has tried every conceivable way to use her voice: big band, symphonies, a cappella, small combos, one instrument, two instruments. She has covered every style as well, everything from classical to country-western. In this quest to keep her musical options open, she had spread herself too thin. Recently, Ethel has begun to realize that her energy has been too diffuse and that perhaps it might work better for her if she began to focus on a specific kind of style, material, or instrumentation. She says, "I think what I have to do now is to intensify my work." Ethel says that while she wants to sing a range of different kinds of songs, she wants them all to be spiritually based.

The album itself was another attempt at independent record production and distribution. ENE virtually produced the album themselves. With assistance from some engineering friends who miked a performance of Ethel's at the Maryland Inn, they produced the master tapes. Around this time the Arnetts also invested in an eight-track system and some other pieces of technical equipment. Their basement took on the appearance of a recording studio.

Commercially the album was less than a break-even investment. Ethel says that they never intended it for wide-scale distribution. In her view, it fit more in the category of a collector's item. Like the other albums, this one didn't contain that elusive magic moment either. However, it was their own production and it was a new beginning toward taking full responsibility for the outcome. Earl's interest in the project was an attempt to discover the ways that the artistic and the business ends could meet on some sort of common ground.

As a Baltimore resident and performer, Ethel Ennis was greatly in demand. She was sought out for benefits, entertainment for political functions, and as a board member for various art organizations and institutions. She also was constantly invited to perform at concerts in areas of the city such as the Inner Harbor and the Mount Royal Station, neighborhoods demonstrating a new-found pride that Baltimoreans were experiencing as the city left the doldrums of *its* past and became hailed as the redevelopment miracle of the East Coast. For most of these functions, Ethel received no financial remuneration. It was her gift to the city.

But there was still a reward for Ethel. These events gave her the local exposure that allowed her to cement her bonds with her own black culture. Ironically, it was Earl who guided Ethel into examining her roots and adopting a more ethnic approach to her work. This expression of Ethel's artistry came to fruition locally when she appeared as the highlight of the 1980 Afram (Afro-American) Festival, part of Baltimore's summer "Showcase of Nations."

Until that event, the black community wasn't really convinced, in Ethel's view, that she was really one of them, not musically that is. "It felt that I wasn't really accepted because the music I was doin' was on the sophisticated side and it was labeled 'white.' I guess I didn't sound like I look and that was the problem. In the *white* world what I got from people was, 'You sound like that, but you look like *this.*' In the black world they were sayin', 'You look like *this,* but you sound like *that.*'"

At Afram, if there ever were any feelings of animosity or envy toward Ethel from her people, the power that she transmitted that evening blew them all to bits. A huge crowd gathered at Rash Field at the new Inner Harbor to experience and share the contributions of the Black American community in Baltimore. Ethel Ennis was the headliner. When she came onstage, she sparkled with the elegance of an African queen. Her hair was braided and beaded and she wore a flowing pristine white pantsuit. Her eyes sparkled and shone. But all of that didn't come close to the loving energy that she transmitted to the crowd. They were, after all, her people, her folks. At one point in the performance, Ethel placed herself on a small stool in the middle of the stage. She picked up her guitar and slowly started strumming some chords accompanied on the violin by former concertmaster of the Baltimore Symphony, Isidor Saslav. The soulful strains began to emanate from her being: "Sometimes I feel like a motherless child. Sometimes I feel like a motherless child. . . ."

As Ethel recalls the moment, "In a way it was the truth, the feeling of being a motherless child. Especially sounding white and bein' married to a white man and yet bein' here with all my people. This time when I sang the song, I felt it should be treated differently; I didn't put it in the jazz idiom. By playing the guitar it was more folky; I didn't try to put any style to it or any label. It was just a simple 'people song.' "

The crowd began to warm up to Ethel. On the heels of "Motherless Child," she delivered another dose of pure Ennis, and in the doing of it she fulfilled yet another part of her past cycle. Against the darkness of the night, a pool of bright light encircled Ethel. The whiteness of her outfit added a mystical touch to the magic of the moment. For an instant there was a pause, and then she found her way into the tune, an old favorite written by the lady who told her personally, "You don't fake . . . keep on singin' that way. . . ." And Ethel kept on singing that way. The tune was "God Bless the Child." The writers were Billie Holiday and Arthur Herzog, Jr. As Ethel sang through the song, the crowd began to groove in on it, and by the time she got to the final bars, they were totally smitten. Perhaps it was the spirit of Billie through Ethel, but it really doesn't matter. Whatever it was it had its own special power. Once again Ethel had reached the hearts of the people—and this time they were her own.

As Ethel says, "That was a revelation—to be accepted musically. That wonderful relationship was terrific. The acceptance was like, 'Thank you. Thank you.' 'Cause they don't have to agree and they don't have to confirm, but they got my truth at that moment and it was recognized."

Earl and Ethel were becoming increasingly absorbed in their commitment to the development of the city. Earl, who wrote about cultural events in the area for the *Sunpapers* felt that the Baltimore-Washington, D.C. corridor was the next cultural mecca on the East Coast. As he discovered the possibilities in the area, he began to develop a theory. It was an extension of Ethel's "stay at home" philosophy. Earl says, "In order to be in the music industry, you've got to get involved in all aspects of it. If you're not prepared to move to New York or Los Angeles, then how can you get involved from a place like Baltimore? The theory we're developing is to create an 'Ethel's Place' and then use the technology that plugs Baltimore into the national entertainment industry."

Clearly the voice had started calling to Earl Arnett. Shortly after the album's release, Earl made a full-time commitment to Ethel's career and resigned from the newspaper. At the time, he didn't quite know how or what they were ultimately going to do or even how they would survive financially. Contrary to public opinion, Ethel is not a wealthy person. After all, how much money could she make on gigs amounting to no more than a total of three or four months work per year and a lot of free benefit concerts? And Earl as a feature writer and local TV critic did not bring in a hefty sum. They managed to live comfortably, but not extravagantly by a long shot. When Earl left the paper, they refinanced the house and then reinvested the money in what was needed to start their new enterprise. The house was turned over to office use. Between the living room and the dining room, they installed a copy machine. The dining room table was given over to Earl's new constant companion, an Olivetti computer.

Shortly before this turn of events, Earl had been approached by Philip Arnoult, the dynamic theater impresario whose Baltimore Theater Project has added a jolt of creative avant garde energy to the city's cultural life. The topic of conversation was Philip's vision of a cabaret theater in the old Heptosoph Hall, which he had been using for his experimental theater ventures since 1971. When the idea was first suggested to Earl, the area around the building was just beginning to come alive. Since then the Mount Royal area has evolved into the city's major cultural center. In fact, its new name is the Mount Royal Cultural Complex. Concentrated in a few square blocks are the sparkling new Meyerhoff Symphony Hall, the newly refurbished Lyric Opera House, and the old B & O railroad station, recently renovated as studios and galleries for the Maryland Institute College of Art.

In addition, each summer for the past three years, the streets have been closed off for one weekend to make room for Artscape. This colorful event, the brainchild of Jody Albright, head of the Mayor's Advisory Committee on Art and Culture, attracts thousands of Baltimoreans to its wide range of offerings. All events are free to the public, and in that sense, as Earl points out, "It is the *first* event of its kind in the nation."

During the course of the weekend, along with the best of Baltimore's outstanding artists in all fields, national stars are also brought in for large-scale outdoor concerts. In 1984, for example, Mercer Ellington, Earl Klugh, and Wynton Marsalis were the headliners.

When Artscape first got off the ground in 1981, the main attraction for the Saturday night concert was Ethel Ennis. She was backed up by a big band led by her sometime musical arranger, talented Gary Dailey, who spent several years on the road with Maynard Ferguson. Ethel's appearance was no accident: Earl Arnett was the producer. He had jockeyed himself into a favorable position as a consultant to the Artscape Board of Directors and had worked out a $10,000 deal with them to finance the above-mentioned concert. The money did not all go to Ethel Ennis. Musicians, technical personnel, and several actors who were involved all received well-earned payment for their services, often a rare event in the world of the arts.

When the idea of the theater cabaret first came to light, the Arnetts did not immediately grab onto it. For one thing, they had no financial reserves to bring it about. Then another offer came, with money available. An investor restauranteur, who had been a fan of Ethel's, suggested that he wanted to open a restaurant in the Inner Harbor area and use Ethel's name as a drawing card. They all tried to make that offer work, but they couldn't reach an agreement. Time passed and Arnoult came around again. This time Earl looked at Philip's idea more seriously and became inspired by it. Starting with nothing more than the dream, Earl has persistently worked through every aspect of the business plan and broken through every obstacle in himself and the circumstances. After three years of planning, negotiating, redesigning, and all the myriad of other twists and turns that are part of real estate development, Ethel's Place is now under construction. Earl explains, "It's the *first* project of its kind in the country. It's a model for innovative cooperation between public and private, profit and non-profit, art and business sectors of a community."

As the financial planning and legal structures have evolved, various people have come and gone. At present, a team of innovative developers with a very successful track record—Bill Struever, Fred Struever, Cobber Eccles, and Ted Rouse—and, of course, Earl and Ethel are the members of the Heptosoph Limited Partnership. This business entity is currently rehabilitating the building and will in turn lease the space to the Baltimore Theater Project and Ethel's Place.

Architect Amy Gould has been retained to design the physical space. Ethel's Place, according to Earl's fact sheet (printed through the Olivetti computer), will be "a multi-level, flexible entertainment and restaurant space. It will feature live music, a lunch and dinner menu with emphasis on fresh specials and first class beverages, and spaces designed to make everyone feel comfortable."

The building will contain a main performance space on the bottom level, with a tiered balcony. It will feature seating for about 200 people and will boast the latest in theatrical lighting and a state-of-the-art sound system. In addition to Ethel's performances at her new home base, other nationally known singers will be booked, as well as the best jazz, pop, and soul musical artists in the Baltimore-Washington area. Plans also include chamber music, bluegrass, big band, and professional cabaret theater.

The design of the facility provides for three main areas: a neighborhood lounge area with graphics reflecting Baltimore's musical and theatrical history; a more formal wood and glass restaurant adjoined by an outdoor cafe; and the cabaret.

The Theater Project upstairs will sport a new look too. Seating will be increased and more comfortable. The lobby will be expanded, and there will be a gallery for art exhibits. These changes will allow Mr. Arnoult to have yet another part of his vision fulfilled. The Theater Project will initiate a new series that will include five international companies, each one in residency for five weeks. There will also be a dance program that will include five modern dance companies. The remainder of the season will be turned over to special events, works in progress, and artists' collaborations.

Altogether the amount of financing on the project is close to two million dollars. Ethel Ennis is majority owner of the business. This, of course, was Earl's doing once again. He has spent countless hours over the past few years studying accounting, financing, and business practices. And so the forces have come full cycle, and with this turn, the last of Miss Rose's predictions has come to pass: the red ace of diamonds is up for Ethel Ennis. And Earl doesn't have to tell us that Ethel Ennis may be the *first* black female entertainer in the US to have the controlling share of such an enterprise.

While the project appears to be ambitious and promising, a slight scent of skepticism pervades the air. There are those who wonder if this is yet another form of the "Red Fox" syndrome, which in many ways kept Ethel from moving on earlier in her career. How will she be able to reach out nationally from the security of her home base? Earl's reply is, "When we know that all of the bugs are worked out of the initial stages of operation, we plan to get involved in using cable TV. We can beam performances from Ethel's Place to other locations throughout the country." All this very strongly states that, for the most part, Ethel Ennis plans to stay home. As Ethel sees it, "The root is here and we can branch out from that. It's like having many spores. Networking gets easier every day. So we'll be consciously expanding from that."

Ethel's excitement about Ethel's Place grows continually as the process moves further along. Every time she and Earl go to a restaurant these days, they are noticing everything about it—silverware, glasses, decor, table-cloths—and they try not to overlook anything. Ethel is especially attentive to the food. The lady is a talented cook. She says, "I like to cook my food with love. I think everything adds to it: the way you chop the food, what you put in it. It's all goin' in your body and it matters what kind of vibes you cook it with." She has even half seriously thought about going into the food products business someday. Perhaps it won't be too long before a loaf of Mother Ethel's homemade bread appears on the shelf at the local supermarket. These days anything seems possible for Ethel.

Despite Ethel's strong preference for operating her career predominately from her new home base, she is not totally adverse to doing a small amount of traveling. Her dream is to someday perform in Brazil. Ethel feels a strong pull toward that part of the world and especially likes to perform tunes with a Latin American beat. She may have her opportunity to get a strong dose of Brazil without ever having to leave this country. In the works at the moment are plans for a Broadway play based on the life of Carmen Miranda. Ethel has been approached to play the second female lead. The music is all Brazilian inspired and is being written by Brazilian composer Luis Bonfa.

Touring internationally is a subject that comes up time and again. Ethel and Earl are in a good position to do this since they are the official Cultural Ambassadors for the City of Baltimore. This honor grew from another seed planted by Philip Arnoult. Arnoult, whose involvement in avant garde theater extends world-wide, suggested to Earl that if Ethel received such an honor, it would give her the opportunity to represent Baltimore here and abroad. It also might be a way to have international tours supported financially by the State Department. This suggestion made sense to Earl; his brother David has served as cultural attache to our embassies in various parts of the world and is now stationed in Turkey. So Earl took the initiative and suggested the idea to the Mayor. The Mayor went for it; he has always been an ardent admirer of Ethel's. In an official presentation at City Hall in February, 1982, Mayor William Donald Schaefer bestowed the honor on the Arnetts, and when Ethel's Place is completed, Earl and Ethel plan to use it as their "cultural embassy."

Clearly Earl's lifestyle since he left the newspaper has shifted dramatically. Earl firmly believes that we all shape our own destinies. In other words, if we want something to come about in our lives, we have to *cause* it to happen, using all of the inner and outer resources at our disposal. This is the flip side of the way that Ethel approached life for most of her years. For Ethel it was all up to God, totally. Now it appears as if there has been a balancing between the two points of view for both of them. Both of them now believe that going out on your own toward your vision can work if one is willing to take the risk and has enough trust, faith, and commitment.

Earl has demonstrated his commitment and has pulled off what looked impossible at the outset. He now perceives himself as the provider of the business and economic foundation of their joint ventures, as well as a producer of theatrical and musical events and the president of the Ethel's Place corporation.

While Earl is moving rapidly toward realizing his dreams, it wasn't always this way. Until recently he spent much of his time wondering what he could do to provide answers for Ethel, particularly in matters where in reality, only Ethel herself could ultimately make the choices. At one point Earl realized that he had done all he could to help Ethel and that she would have to take a stand for herself. Not that he wouldn't be there to encourage and support her, but Earl realized that he couldn't be Ethel— Ethel had to be Ethel. So he gave up some of the shield of protection that he had provided over the years, "the mask against the world" as he referred to it, and in that moment Ethel appeared fully as herself, as her own power. It was now up to Ethel to be and do her own life.

This shift in thinking was Earl's 1984 New Year's gift to Ethel. Since then, she has traveled to New York to talk to a club owner about a booking, a breakthrough for Ethel. Although this attempt didn't work out, other offerings are in the works and look promising for the future. Another very positive move on Ethel's part has been her amicable reconciliation with Gerry Purcell. They had stayed in touch only minimally throughout the years, but recently they set up an appointment while Ethel was in New York. This opened up the relationship for future possibilities, not as it was in the past, but rather in a way in which Purcell would be willing to help the Arnett's ventures in whatever manner he could.

Ironically, just after Purcell was interviewed for this biography, an article written by him appeared in *Variety* for their seventy-eighth anniversary issue (January 11, 1984). Apparently, he also has learned a few tough lessons throughout the years. Speaking on behalf of personal management, Purcell stated in the article:

> In choosing clients, a personal manager should evaluate and place great emphasis on the intelligence and dedication of the artist. Those two traits are more important than talent. Talent can be developed; the others are an essential part of one's character and will contribute toward a mutual and lasting relationship . . . If an artist is not smart enough to know you are important to him, providing you are contributing meaningfully to his success, you are better off without him. . . .

Ethel Ennis well might have been the inspiration for these vital lessons for Gerry Purcell's own development as a strong manager.

In 1973, Ethel established a new home base in the King of France Tavern at the Maryland Inn in Annapolis. Like the Red Fox, this room also was the scene of celebrations like Ethel's forty-sixth birthday *(above)* in 1978.

Ethel *(left)* rehearses at the Maryland Inn for camera crew (not shown) from a local school system.

WILLIAM KLENDER

In 1979, ENE Productions came to life again as Earl and Ethel tried their hand at producing another album recorded live at the Maryland Inn. This one called *Ethel* was engineered by friends from the Maryland Center for Public Broadcasting. Don Barto and Ethel check recording levels *(above)* in a room at the Maryland Inn.

Ethel meets Ethel face-to-face as she autographs the album during an event at the Convention Center in 1980 *(below)*.

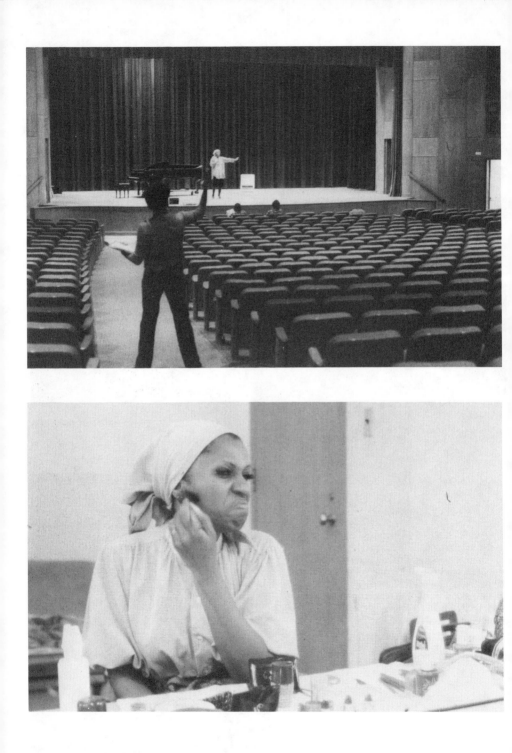

Behind the scenes at a rehearsal in 1980, Director Ed Rosen checks Ethel's staging in Shriver Hall auditorium at Johns Hopkins University *(opposite, top)*. Ethel clowns around in the dressing room as she makes faces in the mirror while putting on make-up *(opposite, bottom)*.

In typical dramatic fashion, Ethel strikes a sophisticated pose while performing a number *(above)*.

WENDELL HOLLAND

Earl and Ethel share an intimate moment at home *(above)* as they read through a script.

Ethel, the nurturing provider, feeds Earl *(opposite, top)*. She loves to cook as much as she loves to sing.

Pianist Mark Cohen rehearses with Ethel in her music room as she studies crib sheets of lyrics taped to the wall *(opposite, bottom)*.

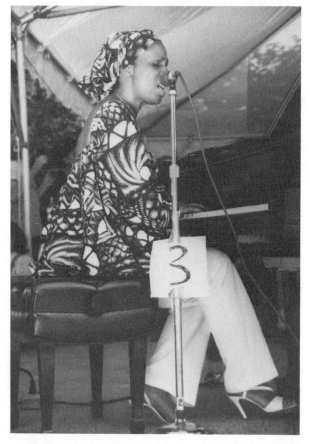

Ethel makes a rest stop (*above*) in 1981 on the way to a jazz festival (*pictured here and on the following page*) held at ballplayer Jackie Robinson's estate. A gathering of jazz greats perform there annually to benefit the Jackie Robinson Scholarship Fund. In a rare performance, Ethel accompanies herself on the piano, something she has done infrequently since the early days of her career (*left*).

Brother Andrew on tenor (*above*) takes a solo while Ethel keeps the beat going with percussionist Gaynell Coburn, currently Miss Wheelchair America. Ethel shares a warm embrace with an old friend, singer Joe Williams. She appeared with him at earlier jazz fests in Newport and Monterey (*right*).

Just as Ethel "sang in" Republican Nixon for his second term in January, 1973, she "sings out" Democrat Carter during last days of his term in January, 1981. This time, however, there was no national exposure as there had been when she sang the anthem, just a quiet little gathering in the White House. Carter is seated at bottom right.

igns of the time on the corners
f Preston and Cathedral Streets
nnounce the coming of Ethel's
lace, a cabaret/theater which
rill be Ethel's permanent home
ase in Baltimore *(right)*. At
roundbreaking ceremonies on
une 21, 1984, Ethel sings her
rst gig on the site of Ethel's
'lace. Building shown directly
cross the street is the new
Meyerhoff Symphony Hall
below).

Ethel, in an intense moment travels deeply within to get to the essence of the song. Her present artistic goal is to sing songs that convey a feeling of spirituality like the words in "Open Your Eyes, You Can Fly"—"Never be afraid to love."

X   ...God Bless the Child

THE climate of America has opened up considerably since the beginning days of Ethel's career in the 1940s, especially regarding our view of the value of contributions made by Black Americans and women. For the first time in American history, we have a female candidate for the office of Vice President of the United States. Although this move may have slight traces of political gimmicry on behalf of the Mondale ticket, nonetheless, it is a strong acknowledgment of the power of women in the US.

Black America, too, has swung out with tremendous impact. At this writing, we are in the last days of the Olympic Summer Games in Los Angeles. Our country has been strongly represented, if not dominated, by the talent of committed black athletes. And as far as the role of blacks in pop music, it's come a long way from "race records" and "the chittlin' circuit" to the current reign of Michael Jackson, the Frank Sinatra of today's generation. Although the votes aren't in yet, Jackson may yet go down in musical history as the catalyst for pop explosion number four. Unlike other superstars, Jackson is clearly in tune with his ultimate musical goal. J. D. Considine spelled it out in an article about Jackson in the *Sunday Sun* (March 4, 1984): "As Mr. Jackson once put it, his major artistic and powerfully ambitious goal is 'to try to integrate all races into one through the love of music.' "

On this purpose, Ethel Ennis and Michael Jackson are fully aligned. The world, it seems, has come full circle in Ethel's favor. Blacks, females, jazz, and spirituality all have found their voice in 1980s America.

And now what—where does Ethel Ennis go from here? Has she truly become clear and let go of those self-defeating attitudes that slowed her down in the past? Is it all right to be a star, to have fame and fortune, to acknowledge her own inner power? Is she aware that her life is her own creation, or is she still going along passively on hit-or-miss random chance? Ethel speaks for herself on these matters:

"I want to be a star, but I want to be the kind of star where the inner being is so clear that you're giving off vibrations like a ball of energy. Like the people don't even see you, they just feel the energy. It's almost like luminous fibers.

"My strong point is my spirituality. How do I market that? I want people to get my message that you have to love yourself first, then the door opens anew. 'Cause when you love yourself, you love God.

"I have a burning desire to sing what I've learned spiritually in the past few years. I want to sing songs that are inner visions, songs of awakening and happy answers of life. I want my songs to have a theme. The theme I want to work with is like the words in 'Open Your Eyes, You Can Fly'—'Never be afraid to love . . . .' I want people to not be afraid to love themselves.

"I want it to be known that I know what's going on in the world—it's spirituality that counts. This society teaches differences; I'm tryin' to say that spiritually we're the same.

"Earl and I have taken our stand that America can be beautiful. It's not that way right now. But we all can be equal. That's what I represent and what I want my music to represent."

To this end, another project in the works is yet another album. Given the track record of the past, has Ethel learned what it would take to make an album that could work? Has she learned what it would take to get that luminous ball of energy out into the universe as far as it can go? At the moment the investors are at work putting together the financial package. Will Ethel Ennis be able to do her part? Does she know this time what it is she really wants to do? Or is she once again waiting for somebody out there to give her answers? Again Ethel speaks for herself:

"This time I'm goin' out with a purpose. I'm singin' *me*, which was never there before. I want to use the tonality with words that are clear, the text has to be very clear. I can write all kinds of songs. I don't have to sing them all, but they have to be sung with spirituality, with an awareness of knowing where the world is now.

"I want to come up with a product that's commercially, politically, and spiritually accepted. And I want to do it *my way* again. This time if it doesn't work, I'll say that I'm responsible. In the past, if it didn't work, I would say, 'Well, it just wasn't meant to be.' But I've let go of that.

"*Commercially* the sound has to be right, that's what makes the money. *Politically* I want people to know that I understand the set up, the program of society. I know what it's all about. I want to say something that expresses tellin' the truth. Therapeutic action is what's needed now. The singer's aware of what's goin' on. And *spiritually* I want to cause the way it's going to be presented. I just want to say, 'Hey, we're all the same. We're all fathered by the same spirit, we're all pieces of it.' I would like the planet aglow, burning in the universe as a *spiritual* ball, not as a glowing mass of destruction where we're all blown to fragments.

"When you can glow with the Energy of Oneness, who knows what that can put out into the universe?"

So as Ethel Ennis enters the prime of her life, the energy around her is aglow with possibility. As she approaches fifty-two, it appears that Ethel

Ennis will fulfill the gift that God blessed her with in the beginning. Sometimes it takes a long time to know that you are God in your universe, just as others are in theirs. We have all got this power and it's up to each one of us to grow it, use it, care for it, and be responsible for our lives in all of their dimensions. Like it or not, we are the only ones on this planet who are capable of evolving human "being" to the next level. Ethel Ennis is doing her part. Honey and Mama are probably up there beaming, "bustin' their buttons." As for the rest of us, stay tuned . . . .

Bibliography

Apel, Willi and Ralph T. Daniel. *The Harvard Brief Dictionary of Music.* New York: Simon and Schuster, Pocket Books, 1960.

Bebey, Francis. *African Music: A People's Art.* Westport: Lawrence Hill and Company, 1975.

Blacking, John. *How Musical Is Man?* Seattle: University of Washington Press, 1973.

Brown, Peter, and Steven Gaines. *The Love You Make: An Insider's Story of The Beatles.* New York: New American Library, Signet Books, 1983.

Collier, James Lincoln. *The Making of Jazz, A Comprehensive History.* Boston: Houghton Mifflin, 1979.

Feather, Leonard. *The Book of Jazz From Then Till Now.* New York: Horizon Press, 1957.

Friedman, Martha. *Overcoming Fear of Success.* New York: Warner Books by arrangement with Seaview Books, 1980.

Gourse, Leslie. *Louis' Children: American Jazz Singers.* New York: William Morrow and Co., Quill, 1984.

Martin, George, with Jeremy Hornsby. *All You Need Is Ears.* New York: St. Martin's Press, 1979.

Middleton, Richard and David Horn, eds. *Popular Music 1: Folk or Popular? Distinctions, Influences, Continuities.* New York: Cambridge University Press, 1981.

Placksin, Sally. *American Women in Jazz: 1900 to the Present.* New York: Wideview Books, 1982.

Roberts, John Storm. *Black Music of Two Worlds.* New York: William Morrow and Co., 1974.

Shaw, Arnold. *Dictionary of American Pop/Rock.* New York: Schirmer Books, 1982.

Shotton, Pete and Nicholas Schaffner. *John Lennon in My Life.* New York: Stein and Day, Scarborough, 1983.

Tame, David. *The Secret Power of Music: The Transformation of Self and Society Through Musical Energy.* New York: Destiny Books, 1984.

Taylor, Paula. *Elvis Presley.* Mankato, Minn.: Creative Education, 1970.

Zalkind, Ronald. *Contemporary Music Almanac, 1980/81.* New York: Schirmer Books, 1980.

Discography

Albums

Ethel Ennis Sings Lullabys for Losers Jubilee, 1955 (5 re-issues, most recent on Columbia Nippon in 1977) LP1021

Change of Scenery Capitol, 1957 T941

Have You Forgotten? Capitol, 1958 T1078

This is Ethel Ennis RCA, 1964 LPM-2786 Stereo LSP-2786

Once Again, Ethel Ennis RCA, 1964 Mono LPM-2862 Stereo LSP-2862

Eyes for You/Ethel Ennis RCA, 1965 Mono LPM-2984 Stereo LSP-2984

Ethel Ennis, My Kind of Waltztime RCA, 1965 Mono LPM-2986 Stereo LSP-2986

Ethel Ennis, God Bless the Child RCA Camden re-issue, 1973 and 1980 ACL 1-0157

Ten Sides of Ethel Ennis BASF, 1973 BB-25121 Stereo

Ethel EnE, 1980 ENE 3113 Stereo

Singles

Jubilee, 1955: "Off Shore," "I've Got You Under My Skin"

Atlantic, 1956: "Pair of Fools," "Got It in My Blood"

Capitol EP, 1957

RCA, 1964: "Boy from Ipanema," "When Will the Hurt be Over?"

RCA, 1964: "Matchmaker," "Now I Have Everything"

RCA, 1964: "For a Little While," "San Juan"

RCA, 1965: "I've Got That Feeling," "About Love"

RCA, 1965: "We Could Learn Together," "Look at Me"

Spiral, 1972: "Who Is It This Time?", "Call Me Young"

Spiral, 1972: "Sing Me a Tune," "I Wonder Who My Daddy Is"

Spiral, 1973: "I Believe in Love," "I Wonder Who My Daddy Is"

SNS, 1976: "Yankee Disco," "America 200"

(from unreleased bicentennial album)

For further information regarding recordings
by Ethel Ennis, please contact:
ENE PRODUCTIONS
3113 LEIGHTON AVENUE
BALTIMORE, MD 21215